D0039611

The Results-Driven Manager Series

The Results-Driven Manager series collects timely articles from *Harvard Management Update* and *Harvard Management Communication Letter* to help senior to middle managers sharpen their skills, increase their effectiveness, and gain a competitive edge. Presented in a concise, accessible format to save managers valuable time, these books offer authoritative insights and techniques for improving job performance and achieving immediate results.

Other books in the series:

Managing Yourself for the Career You Want

Teams That Click

Presentations That Persuade and Motivate

Winning Negotiations That Preserve Relationships

Face-to-Face Communications for Clarity and Impact

A Timesaving Guide

THE RESULTS-DRIVEN MANAGER

Face-to-Face Communications for Clarity and Impact

. . .

Harvard Business School Press

Boston, Massachusetts

No part of this publication may be reproduced, stored in or introduced into a retrieval system, or transmitted, in any form, or by any means (electronic, mechanical, photocopying, recording, or otherwise), without the prior permission of the publisher. Requests for permission should be directed to permissions@hbsp.harvard.edu, or mailed to Permissions, Harvard Business School Publishing, 60 Harvard Way, Boston, Massachusetts 02163.

Library of Congress Cataloging-in-Publication Data

The results-driven manager: face-to-face communications for clarity and impact.
    p.   cm. — (The Results-driven manager series)
    ISBN 1-59139-347-7
    Added t.p. title: Face-to-face communications for clarity and impact. 1. Business communication. 2. Oral communication. 3. Nonverbal communication. 4. Miscommunication. I. Title: Face-to-face communications for clarity and impact. II. Series.
    HF5718.R47 2004
    658.4′52—dc22

                                   2003019039

The paper used in this publication meets the requirements of the American National Standard for Permanence of Paper for Publications and Documents in Libraries and Archives Z39.48-1992.

Contents

Contents

Using Nonverbal Communication

"Reading" Others' Signals

Contents

Face-to-Face
Communications
for Clarity
and Impact

Introduction

. . .

With today's dizzying proliferation of communication technologies—ranging from e-mail and instant messaging to paging and teleconferencing—it's easy to imagine a time when we won't have to meet "in person" to conduct business. Yet face-to-face communication has taken on more importance than ever.

If you have doubts about this, consider the disasters that can erupt when you're communicating with someone else using a less personal vehicle—such as e-mail. A joke or casual remark that might have scored a hit in a face-to-face conversation falls flat in the e-mail or, worse, offends the recipient. A long, dense block of text leaves readers confused or impatient. Nuances in meaning never make the transition from sender to receiver. Perhaps it's not surprising that e-mail users have developed "emoticons," little pictographs comprising combinations of letters and punctuation marks—such as ":-)" to express a

1

smile or ":O" to express alarm or surprise. Emoticons provide a personal touch to an otherwise impersonal mode of communication—revealing our deep reliance on emotion in our exchanges with one another.

But even when we do communicate face to face with others, plenty can still go wrong. Consider a performance evaluation with an employee that turns disastrous, or a workplace relationship increasingly racked by tension even though we don't know why. Or what about a troubling misunderstanding over who had agreed to do what on a big project—even though people seemed so clear about their responsibilities during the meeting?

Business mishaps owing to faulty face-to-face communications are legion—from a team whose members drag their feet in carrying out an assignment, to an inability to get the support you need from a colleague, to the discovery that someone you thought of as trustworthy actually isn't.

Given the gravity of these scenarios, it's clear that any manager's career hinges on his or her ability to master the art of face-to-face communication. And this form of encounter grows more crucial every day. Why? In today's "flattened" organizations, managers must resort to means other than command-and-control to win support for their ideas. That means influencing people over whom they have no formal authority. To cultivate interpersonal influence, we have to get to know other managers—something that requires lots of face-to-face communication. This "old-fashioned" form of communication thus provides a crucial source of power in a manager's arsenal of influence.

Moreover, in the age of global-business, many companies' workforces, customers, and partnering organizations are increasingly diverse. With diversity come more opportunities for misunderstandings between managers. Again, face-to-face encounters can help conversation participants better understand one another's perspectives.

Finally, face-to-face communication continues to serve a central role in business interactions for the simple reason that we're animals: We make decisions based just as much on emotion as on reason. For example, when we meet someone new, we work to determine how trustworthy or powerful that person is, whether we share common interests and friends, whether we like him or her. Communicating face to face conveys rich information about these emotional aspects of human interaction.

Skilled face-to-face communicators achieve astonishing outcomes that benefit themselves and their companies. Here are just a few examples of what you can accomplish by communicating effectively with colleagues, employees, customers, business partners—indeed, anyone with whom you interact during a typical workday:

- You persuade a key decision maker to accept and support your new idea.

Introduction

- You inspire your team to follow your lead in launching a change initiative.

- You gain information with which to assess what's going on with a difficult project.

- You diagnose problems in the way your unit is operating.

- You help generate creative, out-of-the-box thinking among employees working on a complex program.

- You convince people of the merits of embracing a challenging new vision or mission.

- You deliver constructive criticism to a direct report or business partner without triggering defensiveness.

- You soothe an irate customer, preventing the tension from escalating to damaging levels.

- You detect dishonesty in a supplier's rep who is attempting to sell you a new contract.

So it's clear that mastery of face-to-face communication counts among the most vital of managerial talents. But what is face-to-face communication, exactly? What does it consist of, and how do we know when we're engaging in it?

The Nature of Face-to-Face Communication

Any face-to-face exchange between people entails a bewildering array of behaviors and information—everything from the spoken word to nonverbal signals. Examples of communication through the spoken word might include questioning, making statements, and modulating voice tone and volume. Nonverbal signals may entail facial expressions, gestures, and body posture: The wideness of a listener's eyes, whether a speaker is staring at the audience or looking away, smiling versus not smiling—all of these constitute additional examples of nonverbal communication that impart vital information about participants' emotions and thoughts.

There's no doubt about it: Face-to-face communication is complex. Moreover, the rules governing this kind of interpersonal exchange can prove contradictory. Plenty of experts have offered suggestions for deciphering others' agendas and states of mind during a face-to-face encounter—only to see their advice shot down by colleagues who have a totally different view on the subject.

For instance, as Nick Morgan asks in the article "The Truth Behind the Smile and Other Myths," should we "steeple" our fingers—or not—to show we're intelligent during a meeting? Views on the meaning of this behavior have changed over the years. And should we conclude that a person who can't seem to look us in the eye while we're talking is lying? Or might he or she be experiencing some other emotion that has nothing to do with honesty? Again, the truth about this behavior seems more complex than we originally believed.

Yet despite these complexities, we can learn to become more effective at face-to-face communication. And we should—if we hope to get the results we desire in a rapidly changing business environment.

So what's the best way to hone your communication talent? This volume helps you by breaking the task into four major themes:

- Discover how to use the spoken word effectively.

- Use nonverbal communication thoughtfully.

- Learn how to "read" others' signals during a face-to-face exchange.

- Master the challenge of communicating effectively under pressure—when opportunities for misunderstandings become especially pronounced.

Let's take a closer look at each of these below.

Using the Spoken Word Effectively

The articles in the first part of this volume focus on ways to use the spoken word skillfully during face-to-face encounters with others in the workplace. As Betty A. Marton explains in "Mastering the Art of Persuasion," communicators increase their effectiveness most when they strive for "social power"—influence that enables them to enhance a group's success by emphasizing shared objectives.

In the same article, Marton describes five suggestions offered by management expert Jay Conger for cultivating your social power:

1. Connect emotionally with others by demonstrating your own commitment to your position, and adjust the tone and approach of your argument to your audience's emotional state.

2. Find the common ground shared by you and your audience by listening carefully to their concerns and adapting your message accordingly.

3. Use vivid language (stories, anecdotes) and *compelling evidence* (authoritative sources) in delivering your message—because listeners absorb information in direct proportion to its vividness.

4. Establish your credibility by making—and then fulfilling—commitments and cultivating trusting relationships both within and beyond your organization.

5. Become an effective team builder by taking workshops in group processing and from running

small groups—which involves both giving meaningful content and getting feedback.

In "How to Bring About Change by Paying Attention
to What You and Others Say," Loren Gary shares insights from several books about language and power.
For example, Sarah Myers McGinty, in Power Talk: Using
Language to Build Authority and Influence, encourages
managers to select from two different communication
modes, depending on the situation. To lead people
through stressful times, McGinty advises, use "language
from the center"—making authoritative statements, challenging others' claims, and controlling the conversation
flow. To gather information and encourage exploration
and collaboration, use "language from the edge"—asking
questions, getting other speakers involved, keeping communication channels open.

Gary also presents suggestions that Robert Kegan and
Lisa Laskow Lahey offer in their book *How the Way We
Talk Can Change the Way We Work: Seven Languages for
Transformation*. These authors recommend using "the
language of public agreement" to break down organizational "immune systems" that conspire to maintain the
status quo. For example, managers can encourage their
team members to forge a simple agreement that "We will
all speak directly to one another when problems arise."
Though this agreement won't eradicate the problem of
people talking behind each other's backs, its mere exis-
tence, the authors explain, "creates the possibility of a

violation, so that when someone breaks the agreement, there is now the opportunity to examine what caused it."

In "How to Make Your Case in 30 Seconds or Less," Nick Wreden shifts gears from spoken communication techniques that require longer-term cultivation to tactics that you use when you have just seconds or minutes to convey a message orally. Wreden cites the all-important "elevator pitch," which "gets its name from the 30-second opportunity to tell—and sell—your story during a three- or four-story elevator ride." A well-crafted elevator pitch can help you communicate effectively in a wide range of circumstances, such as "job interviews, networking events, public relations opportunities, presentations to executives, and sales. . . ." Key tips for formulating your pitch include knowing your goal (to get permission to phone the other person? to be able to send additional information?), knowing your subject, understanding your audience's needs, and organizing your pitch so that it closes with a request to take the next step in the relationship.

John Baldoni explores a different component of the spoken word in "Are You Asking the Right Questions?" In this article, he maintains that posing the right questions at the right time "can be a powerful tool to help managers explore, discover, and illuminate—and help their employees achieve new levels of productivity." By presenting questions in a nonthreatening way, you facilitate employees' learning by stimulating self-reflection. Your payoff? Better performance in the future.

How do you know what types of questions to ask, and when? That depends on the stage of a project or initiative. For example, early in an effort, find out what's going on "in the trenches" by asking what's uppermost in employees' minds. Later, inspire people to reach for greater performance by asking them what they're capable of—and what stretch goals they may want to embrace.

The final article in this section—"Is One-Dimensional Communication Limiting Your Leadership?" by Theodore Kinni—explores the idea that verbal communication takes place through three channels: factual, emotional, and symbolic. The best face-to-face communicators, Kinni writes, don't rely on facts alone to convey their message. Instead, they interpret data—explaining what it means to them and why the information is important to listeners. They also use emotion to amplify their communications—sharing their own feelings with their audience and telling stories and anecdotes that enable them to connect with listeners on an emotional level. Skilled communicators also leverage the power of symbols— which can take the form of ceremonies; awards; logos; and songs, poems, or quotes that have profound meaning for listeners.

Using Nonverbal Communication

In face-to-face communication, nonverbal signals are just as powerful as—if not more powerful than—the spo-

ken word. Indeed, some studies suggest that when a
speaker's words and body language seem to be conveying
conflicting information, listeners will pay more attention to the nonverbal signals than to the spoken words.
Like other actions and behaviors that constitute nonverbal communication, listening can send a powerful
message. Careful listening keeps the lines of communication open, preventing the misunderstandings that can
damage relationships and lead to finger-pointing. The
article "How to Listen" lays out key guidelines for prac-
ticing this delicate art—such as holding serious conversations in conference rooms, where there will be fewer
distractions; arriving at meetings early to get into a
frame of mind that allows you to concentrate on the
meeting; observing yourself during conversations to
ensure that you're not talking a lot more than the other
person; and demonstrating that you're paying attention
to other conversation participants—for example, by asking clarifying questions.

In "The Truth Behind the Smile and Other Myths,"
Nick Morgan shares the latest challenges to long-
enduring beliefs about what various types of body language mean. For example, it turns out that steady eye
contact isn't necessarily an accurate measure of sincerity
or truthfulness—pathological liars excel at making eye
contact that appears sincere. And whereas many of us
have been told that putting our hands behind our back
conveys a sense of power, most people perceive speakers
who hide their hands as untrustworthy. Morgan dispels

myths about other forms of body language as well—such as touching, smiling, raising one's voice, and talking fast.

Morgan then turns our attention to bodily stance in "Are You Standing in the Way of Your Own Success?" In this selection, he describes 10 ways to use posture to increase your attractiveness, garner respect, and persuade others to take you seriously. Morgan's advice covers numerous aspects that all contribute to posture—such as eye contact, facial expression, head movements, gestures, proximity to your listeners, touch, dress, and physical condition.

The article "What Your Face Reveals and Conceals" emphasizes the importance of conveying emotion skillfully through your own facial expressions and learning how to interpret others' expressions. For example, you can show interest by widening your eyes, express surprise by raising your eyebrows, and convey good and bad feelings by smiling or frowning, respectively. And you can interpret others' facial signals by, for example, watching for expressions that linger for a long period of time—which often signals insincerity. Mastering the "unspoken language of the face" is harder than many people might think—though practice can help.

"Reading" Others' Signals

The articles in this section take the subject of reading others' communications to the next level. In "Get

Around Resistance and Win Over the Other Side," Liz Simpson explains what to do when an opponent digs in his or her heels and refuses to embrace your idea or proposal. Your response? "Be absolutely committed to understanding the other side's position as well as your own." Try on the other person's argument, using the insights you gain to move him or her to your side. And pay attention to the other party's emotions—discerning whether he or she dislikes your idea or you. All of this requires careful listening and questioning—skills that serve you well in any face-to-face encounter.

The selection "How Can You Tell When Your Teammate Is Lying?" provides additional guidelines for detecting dishonesty in others. The best signs of lying show up in the voice and the body. For example, "People pause more, and commit more speech errors, when they are lying than when they are not. Furthermore, their voices tend to rise in pitch—a sign of stress." Of course, to detect these clues, you have to know what someone sounds like when he or she isn't lying. Thus "you'll have more luck spotting liars among the teammates you know well."

The final article in this section—"How to Speedread People"—puts interpretation of others' communications in the context of the Myers-Briggs Type Indicator. This personality test places people along four continua: extraversion-introversion, sensing-intuition, thinking-feeling, and judging-perceiving. The article offers tips for spotting the differences between types and adapting your communication style to each type. For example, extraverts tend to be physical—waving their hands to make points, and displaying lots of emotional range. Introverts are more restrained physically, and project calm and reserve. To communicate most effectively with extraverts, provide a variety of topics to keep them engaged. With introverts, spend more time listening than talking.

Communicating Under Pressure

This section addresses a serious challenge in face-to-face communication: how to manage conversations in stressful, high-pressure circumstances. Such conversations might unfold in situations in which stress, regardless of its source, impairs our ability to communicate clearly or concentrate during a meeting. Or perhaps a person we're talking with becomes angry during the conversation, or we're struggling to deliver constructive criticism to someone we believe won't take it well.

Whatever the circumstance, managers need a special set of tools for communicating under pressure. Anne Field, in "Don't Let Stress Strain Communication," offers guidelines for avoiding stress-induced conversation disasters. For example, if you're highly stressed, keep your messages short and clear. Encourage others to ask questions. Use the more neutral "I" instead of "you" (which can convey a message of blame), and take conscious steps to slow down conversations.

In "Managing Anger," Richard Bierck explains how to defuse the wrath that can arise owing to delivery of painful criticism or some other hard-to-hear news. Bierck advises lowering the physical manifestations of anger by inviting an irate person to sit down or offering a drink of water. He also suggests communicating nonverbally that you are indeed listening—which you can do with an act as simple as abstaining from interrupting. You can further demonstrate that you're listening by summarizing the other person's thoughts in your own words.

In "When the Direct Approach Backfires, Try Indirect Influence," Martha Craumer points out the pressure involved in influencing others over whom you have no formal authority. She describes six alternatives to giving a directive—including listening more ("people are less apt to put up resistance when they feel you've taken the time to listen to and really understand their issues and concerns"); playing up similarities and mutual contacts (which boosts the odds that the other person will like you); and using appropriate humor to create a common bond.

The article "Is There Any Good Way to Criticize Your Coworkers?" wraps up this section by exploring what many managers consider the most challenging face-to-face communication task of all: delivering critical feedback to others. Three steps can help you tackle this dreaded responsibility:

1. Plan your criticism—noting what you want to change in the other person and what you want to accomplish during the conversation.

2. Seek to improve the other person's behavior or performance, rather than blame him or her for problems that have cropped up.

3. Protect the other person's self-esteem. Additional tips include the following: Be clear about what changes you want to see the person make, and provide critical feedback as soon as possible after an undesirable incident. Explain what rewards will come with improved behavior or perform- ance, and follow up on what happens after the conversation.

Though face-to-face communication remains a com- plex and, in many ways, mysterious aspect of business, it's also one of the most powerful ways to get the results you desire. By skillfully using a combination of the spo- ken word and nonverbal communication, learning to read others' signals, and equipping yourself to communicate in highly stressful situations, you can begin shaping face-to-face encounters for your—and your company's— advantage.

Using the Spoken Word Effectively

• • •

The spoken word constitutes a major component of face-to-face communication. By using words effectively, you can acquire significant personal influence and persuade others to support your ideas and follow your lead on vital change initiatives. But leveraging the spoken word skillfully entails more than just selecting the right terms. It often means connecting on an emotional level with others, using powerful analogies, and posing the right questions at the right time.

The five articles in this section explore each of these complex aspects of the spoken word, providing the thinking behind the advice and a wealth of easy-to-learn techniques for applying powerful principles of speech.

Mastering the Art of Persuasion

• • •

Betty A. Marton

Are you a Donald Trump or a Mahatma Gandhi? Both have reputations as highly persuasive leaders, but with very different operating styles. Richard Boyatzis, professor of organizational behavior at Case Western Reserve University Weatherhead School of Management, defines two distinct drives for power: personalized power, or seeking influence for purely personal gain (the Trump kind); and socialized power, which is used to enhance the success of a group with shared objectives (the Gandhi variety).

If you are going to be a persuasive leader—and wield power effectively—you need to be clear about which model you choose to emulate. And there are consequences; the two models are not equally effective.

"Ask yourself why you are trying to exercise influence," Boyatzis suggests. "Research shows that those whose drive is toward socialized power are the ones who make the most effective leaders, the ones who get promoted over the long term. The drive for personalized power often achieves short-term success, but then blows out."

What You Can Do

Once you know whether you're more Gandhi or Trump, there are specific things you can do that will set you on the path of effective leadership and mastery of the art of persuasion.

Connect Emotionally

Good persuaders use emotions in two crucial ways, writes Jay Conger in an article in *Harvard Business Review* ("The Necessary Art of Persuasion," May–June 1998). They feel their commitment to the position they are advocating in their heart, mind, and gut and are able to show that to others. They also have a strong and accurate sense of their audience's emotional state and adjust the tone and approach of their argument accordingly.

"In the business world, we like to think that our colleagues use reason to make their decisions," he writes.

"Yet if we scratch below the surface, we will always find emotions at play."

But before you can connect with others, you need to understand yourself. "Try first to know what your strengths and limits are," advises Daniel Goleman, author of *Primal Leadership*. "Get feedback from people you work with who know you well. You'll find a difference between what you think you're good at and what others think you're good at."

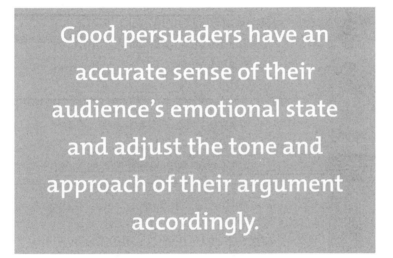

Good persuaders have an accurate sense of their audience's emotional state and adjust the tone and approach of their argument accordingly.

Developing self-awareness takes time. In order to find out how you really feel about things that are going on in your business day, take regular time-outs from everyday stress. You can view these times as a gift you give yourself each day—in the shower, driving to work, during a lunch-hour walk. Wherever you find the time, nothing can replace the insights gained during periods of quiet reflection.

Persuasive Conversations

"All leaders talk," says Philip J. Harkins, president of Linkage, Inc., a Lexington, Mass.-based organizational development company, and author of *Powerful Conversations: How High Impact Leaders Communicate*. Harkins describes leadership itself as a series of conversations—with colleagues, employees, stockholders, the media—anyone who could influence the success or failure of a business.

Harkins argues that leaders should make sure that every conversation they have results in three outcomes: advancement of an agenda, shared learning, and a stronger relationship.

- **Advancement of an agenda.** Harkins says that leaders who begin with an honest expression of their concerns will be able to avoid conversations that don't go anywhere and waste everyone's time. The key is to express your need in both emotional and intellectual terms as a need you have, not as a problem that the other party has. Don't throw blame around, in other words, because that just makes people defensive. Rather, tell them where

Find the Common Ground

Frame your position so it appeals strongly to the people you want to persuade. You can do this by knowing what they are thinking and what their concerns are. This requires not being so intent on getting your own message out that you fail to listen to what is being said.

you're coming from. It's the difference between "I need to be able to figure out how we can meet our quotas next quarter," and "you screwed up—you missed the quotas."

- **Shared learning.** A conversation that has begun honestly has the chance to involve a real exchange of insights. That takes work on both sides—both sides have to be willing to open their minds and learn a little. If quotas were missed, then the employee needs to understand the importance of making them the next time, but you need to understand the reasons behind the unfulfilled quotas. Maybe the employee isn't getting the support she needs to accomplish her goals.

- **Stronger relationships.** A conversation that has begun honestly and has involved shared learning will foster stronger relationships among the parties involved. This stronger relationship in turn can make it easier to have a powerful conversation the next time. Harkins' insight is that honesty is the basis of these favorable outcomes. And honesty begets trust—the basic condition for successful leadership of any kind.

"Watch Kenneth Branagh in *Henry V*," suggests Murray M. Dalziel, global managing director of Organizational Effectiveness and Management Development Services for the Hay Group (Philadephia). "Henry dresses up as a foot soldier, wanders around to campfires, and constructs his speech out of what he learns there."

The best communicators, according to Goleman, have the ability to put aside their internal preoccupations and listen clearly to the concerns of others. "Developing empathy so that you can accurately perceive how others feel is a huge advantage when it comes to persuading them to your way of seeing things," he said.

Develop Your Communication Skills

Use vivid language and compelling evidence to reinforce your position. According to Conger, research shows that listeners absorb information in proportion to its vividness. Learn to give better presentations by taking acting lessons and presentation workshops.

"Think of every conversation as a dramatic presentation," says Boyatzis. "You don't excite people by giving them factual answers."

Have a wide range of strategies and tools that you can use to get your point across, such as stories, anecdotes, and authoritative sources. Be sensitive to when one approach isn't working, so you can switch to another.

Establish Your Credibility

"Research shows," writes Conger, "that most managers are in the habit of overestimating their own credibility—often considerably." The cornerstones of credibility are expertise and relationships built on trust, according to Harry Mills, author of *Artful Persuasion: How to Command Attention, Change Minds, and Influence People*. When leaders lack them, Mills says, "we discount everything they say." How do you establish trust? By making commitments and fulfilling them. For Mills, trust begins with the "law of candor." He advises telling the truth—suitably packaged, of course, but the truth nonetheless.

> "Think of every conversation as a dramatic presentation. You don't excite people by giving them factual answers."

Establish trusting relationships by networking both within and beyond your organization. Join community groups and professional organizations to build your networking skills. People need to feel you care about them and their growth. Become a mentor—get involved in coaching and counseling others.

Become an Effective Team Builder

Practice running small groups with meaningful content. Take workshops in group processing and get feedback in all settings. "Every time you're in a group setting, part of your job is to make sure people are inspired, involved, committed to something important," Boyatzis emphasizes. It's also useful to know how to build a coalition of

25

The Seven Triggers of Persuasion

How do you make conversations persuasive? Harry Mills, chief executive of The Mills Group, a New Zealand training company, and author of *Artful Persuasion: How to Command Attention, Change Minds, and Influence People,* identifies seven "triggers" of persuasion for leaders to use. "Humans are mental misers," says Mills. "When we are rushed or pressured, we like to conserve our energies by using simple rules of thumb to make decisions." By understanding the seven triggers, leaders can align their efforts at persuasion with the way the mind works.

- **Contrast.** Because all judgment is relative, Mills says, use contrast to make your argument appealing. Establish a benchmark, one that lets your proposal show up in a favorable light. If you're trying to persuade your executive team that a round of layoffs is a reasonable step, for example, mention other companies that had to lay off many thousands more workers.
- **Reciprocation.** Most people feel that if they have been given something, they should give something in return. Thus, wise leaders are first givers, then takers. Always be ready with the first concession in a negotiation. Cooperate in little things, so that you can win the big reciprocation.

- **Commitment and Consistency.** Get small initial commitments. You will bind your team in a web of commitment that will ultimately extend to the larger issues. People like to believe that they are behaving consistently, so establishing a consistent pattern of commitment is essential. Smart facilitators know this and get negotiating parties to agree on the ground rules first, both to have the rules and to establish the pattern of agreement.
- **Authority.** Leaders are naturally given the authority that comes with the position. It is yours to keep or to lose. Dress and act the part.
- **Scarcity.** We naturally want things that we perceive to be scarce. Cultivate this sense of scarcity in your employees by creating a vision of the company as unique, something rare, and difficult to achieve.
- **Conformity.** While most of us prefer to think otherwise, the urge to conform or to be part of a successful team is strong in most people. Enlist your employees to your cause, not by asking them to join you, but by asking them to join the team of successful people that you are leading.
- **Liking.** We naturally want to associate with people that we like. Stress the similarities you have with your team, and look for ways to build bridges to them through social occasions that play up those similarities.

support so you know who to go to when you need to make a pitch.

Learn to Negotiate and Manage Conflict

According to Boyatzis, a course in alternative dispute resolution can develop the skills to help people in the middle of conflict. "This is a very sophisticated skill, especially if your emotions are aroused and you need to calm everybody down," he says.

What Not to Do

According to Dalziel, it is difficult for most managers to remember that they are no longer the "hands-on" people they may have once been.

"As a leader, you can no longer directly affect outcomes," he explains. "You can only affect the people who affect the outcomes by inspiring, energizing, and making others feel strong and capable."

Jay Conger has also defined four common mistakes to avoid when trying to persuade others to your point of view.

1. Avoid the Hard Sell

A strong position at the start gives potential opponents something to fight against. Rather, present your position with finesse and reserve.

2. Compromise

Persuasion is a process of give-and-take. People need to know that a persuader is open to their concerns. In addition, compromise can often lead to more sustainable shared solutions.

3. Don't Confuse Argument with Persuasion

Arguing your position is only one part of effective persuasion. You still need to rely on such other tactics as connecting emotionally and communicating effectively.

4. Persuasion Is Not a One-Shot Effort

Persuasion is a process that involves listening, testing a position, compromising, and more. It is not an event. It can be slow and difficult, but it's worth the effort.

For Further Reading

Artful Persuasion: How to Command Attention, Change Minds, and Influence People by Harry Mills (2000, AMACOM, 240 pp.)

Powerful Conversations: How High Impact Leaders Communicate by Philip J. Harkins (1999, McGraw Hill, 192 pp.)

Primal Leadership by Daniel Goleman, Richard Boyatzis, and Annie McKee (2002, HBS Press, 336 pp.)

Reprint C0007B

How to Bring About Change by Paying Attention to What You and Others Say

• • •

Loren Gary

The British novelist and essayist George Orwell got it half right when he wrote, "Good prose is like a window pane." Granted, the more lucid the language, the sharper our understanding of what's being communicated. But words also frame and shape what we see. The ability to notice and use language—at the word level and also at the larger, context-shaping level—constitutes an aspect of leadership that's often overlooked. Three books explore different facets of this idea, highlighting ways in which you can bring awareness to the way you and your colleagues talk and thereby expose the anxieties, hidden commitments, and contradictions that prevent real change from happening.

Using Verbal Patterns to Alter the Balance of Power

"The intersections of speech and social convention" constitute fertile soil for sowing the seeds of change, writes Sarah Myers McGinty, a supervisor in the teacher education program at the Harvard Graduate School of Education, in *Power Talk*. "All day long, we create power and credibility with our performance, with work *and* words." As a manager, you must constantly "sort out the power structures and decide whether you are best served by taking control, directing the conversation, and claiming the right to do so—or by listening, asking questions, and teasing out and collecting the power of ideas." In essence, you must determine which of two basic modes of communication best suits the situation you're facing:

"Language from the Center"

This speech style takes the lead instead of responding to someone else's initiative. It makes authoritative state-

31

ments, contradicts, argues, and controls the flow of conversation. It uses analogies and facts instead of personal stories to make its points. "As work and status progress, Language from the Center becomes increasingly important," writes McGinty. "You can't move up and on without authority."

"Language from the Edge"

This kind of speech responds rather than directs. It asks questions that gather information, gets the other speaker involved, avoids open argument, keeps channels of communication open, and uses protective disclaimers ("This may not be relevant but . . ." or "Maybe I'm being paranoid here but . . ."). This mode conveys exploration and collaboration, personal warmth and approachability. "This is the consultant looking for input and ideas rather than the new CEO, full of declarations and decisions. It's the boss who's willing to listen, the team leader willing to share the power," writes McGinty.

Both modes are necessary, but Language from the Center is often more important when you're trying to lead people through stressful times, says McGinty. One of the people she profiles, Cynthia Danaher, became head of Hewlett-Packard's medical products group at a challenging time in the unit's history. Danaher began her tenure by emphasizing Language from the Edge: she talked about how excited she was by the opportunity and admitted that she was a bit frightened by it as well.

She soon realized that employees wanted her to present a compelling vision and authoritative plans that addressed their concerns and moved the entire group to a better place. Language from the Center may cause some people to leave—but that is occasionally necessary. And it can also carry a personal price. "The power it conveys sets a speaker apart," writes McGinty. "Where there is authority, there is sometimes resentment and usually singularity, perhaps unwelcome isolation."

Creating Minitransformations Through Public Agreement

The way you communicate affects the way you're perceived. Similarly, how you talk to yourself, in those running dialogues you carry on in your head, shapes your attitudes about the world and yourself (see sidebar). But beyond a focus on vocabulary or the choice of particular words, there is another dimension to talk: the way it can either impede or promote organizational learning.

The workplace functions as a language community, observe Robert Kegan and Lisa Laskow Lahey, respectively the William and Miriam Meehan Professor of Adult Learning and Professional Development and research director of the Change Leadership Project at the Harvard Graduate School of Education. "We build strong connections—or fail to—in part through the fairly subtle language forms we use," says Kegan. "As a leader, you

Listening to Your Self-Talk— and Relaxing into Anxiety

"Many current therapies are directed primarily toward reducing stress and anxiety," writes Concord, Mass.-based psychotherapist Robert Gerzon in *Finding Serenity in the Age of Anxiety*. "But if anxiety is life being aware of its own aliveness, then the only way to reduce our anxiety is to become less alive, to numb ourselves to life." Instead, he argues, the challenge is not so much to make anxiety go away as it is to get it working for you.

To do that, you have to become, well, less anxious about your anxieties—you have to learn to relax in their presence enough to be able to hear what they're telling you. Pay attention to your self-talk, that running dialogue that you carry on in your head during most of your waking moments. What can those conversations tell you about how you're feeling about yourself, your professional relationships, and the kind of work that's most meaningful to you? The details contain clues about the anxieties that are gripping you. Once you've recognized the nature of the anxiety, you're better equipped to respond.

Handling anxiety is the key to psychological change, Gerzon continues, but the serenity that results is not some static state of bliss. "Serenity, derived from a Latin word meaning clarity, results from seeing life clearly, without our usual filters," he writes. "Anxiety accompanies the disequilibrium of change." Listening and responding to anxiety must always be "a dynamic, evolving process."

preside over these language communities. You have a choice of whether to be mindful of them—if you're not, you're essentially ratifying the existing language forms." Thus, if you allow established language forms such as complaint and the depreciation of others to go unchecked in the workplace, issues of unfairness, inattentiveness, and ineffectiveness will begin to crop up. "If you go into a company that lacks integrity," says Kegan, "you'll find narratives about all three of these": people in the lower levels of the organization feeling they have a better handle on things than management, or symptoms of organizational disease going unnoticed. Unless they're altered, the existing language forms prevent positive change from happening. The goal of what Kegan and Lahey call "the language of public agreement" is precisely this: to break down the larger organizational immune system that conspires to maintain the status quo.

The quality of agreement in most organizations is extraordinarily thin, note Kegan and Lahey in *How the Way We Talk Can Change the Way We Work*. For instance, it's almost universally agreed that the preferred method of handling a problem you have with someone is to approach the person directly instead of talking to others behind that person's back. Yet very few groups turn this belief into a public agreement. "In most organizations, instead of broad agreements, all you have are individuals' notions of what constitutes decent conduct—but such private notions are always insufficient," says Kegan. "So in our work with teams, the challenge is to forge

agreements that build an organic sense of integrity—
an organizational capacity to lift people up when they
stray across a company boundary or value and gently
place them back into the fold, as you would with a
puppy that strays."

Even a single agreement can have a significant impact.
Let's say that your team members all agree to speak
directly to one another when problems arise. Obviously,
this agreement won't eradicate the problem of people
talking behind each other's backs. But the mere exis-
tence of the agreement creates the possibility of a violation, so that when someone breaks the agreement, there
is now the opportunity to examine what caused it.

In most instances, the person violates the agreement
because of another underlying commitment—for example, the desire to be seen as a compassionate listener and
a trusted source of advice. That competing commitment, laudable as it is, serves as an impediment to the
organizational integrity that the original agreement
seeks to build. "The workplace is filled with these kinds
of contradictions between our commitments, but they
tend to be kept invisible," says Kegan. People aren't even
aware of what their competing commitments are and
how they undermine group trust and performance. Only
if they're brought to the surface and examined can the
contradictions become opportunities for learning.

People often try to build organizational integrity
"through top-down interventions or private conversations," says Kegan, "but these methods have limited

effect." The organizational immune system remains intact, enabling the contradictions between employees' competing commitments to stay invisible. But when a public agreement is in place and a team member confronts you for talking behind someone's back, what you experience is not simply the personal integrity of the person who's confronting you but the integrity of the organization—it's the organization that's reframing your behavior, bringing you back within the bounds of acceptable behavior.

This is not a quick-fix process. "When you try to solve things too quickly, you can be reasonably sure that you'll be the same person at the other end of the process," says Kegan. "By scrutinizing the language of your commitments and the contradictions between the commitments you make, you uncover good problems—problems that, if you stay with them, create opportunities for people to grow and change."

For Further Reading

Power Talk: Using Language to Build Authority and Influence by Sarah Myers McGinty (2001, Warner Books)

How the Way We Talk Can Change the Way We Work: Seven Languages for Transformation by Robert Kegan and Lisa Laskow Lahey (2001, Jossey-Bass)

Finding Serenity in the Age of Anxiety by Robert Gerzon (1998, Bantam Books)

Reprint U0201D

How to Make
Your Case in
30 Seconds
or Less

• • •

Nick Wreden

In 1994, Barnett Helzberg, Jr. was walking by The Plaza
Hotel in New York City when he heard a woman hail
Warren Buffett. Helzberg approached the legendary
investor and said, "Hi, Mr. Buffett. I'm a shareholder in
Berkshire Hathaway and a great admirer of yours. I
believe that my company matches your criteria for
investment."

"Send me more details," Buffett replied. A year later, Helzberg sold his chain of 143 diamond stores to Buffett. Helzberg's story is a classic example of a powerful elevator pitch. An elevator pitch gets its name from the 30-second opportunity to tell—and sell—your story during a three- or four-story elevator ride. The 30-second parameter is based on the typical attention span, according to the book *How to Get Your Point Across in 30 Seconds or Less* by Milo O. Frank. It's one reason why the standard commercial or television "sound bite" lasts 30 seconds.

While elevator pitches are often associated with funding requests, they can be valuable every day. Job interviews, networking events, public relations opportunities, presentations to executives, and sales all demand the ability to successfully deliver a quick and concise explanation of your case.

A 30-second elevator speech quickly demonstrates that you know your business and can communicate it effectively. Yes, a lot of important facts may be left out, but today everyone is skilled at judging relevancy and making decisions with incomplete data. In fact, 15 seconds can be more powerful than 30 seconds. "The more succinct you are, the more successful you will be," says Dr. Alan Weiss, president of Summit Consulting Group in East Greenwich, R.I.

The secret of strong elevator pitches consists of grabbing the attention of listeners, convincing them with the promise of mutual benefit, and setting the stage for follow-up. Speak in terms your audience can relate to.

And communicate with the passion that comes from knowing that this opportunity may never come again. How often do you see Warren Buffett on the street?

Key Tips for Strong Pitches

Know the Goal

The goal of an elevator pitch is not to get funding, a job, or project sign-off. It's to get approval to proceed to the next step, whether it's accepting a phone call, a referral to the right person, or a chance to send additional information. Says Ken Yancey, the CEO of SCORE, an SBA resource partner made up of retired and active volunteers who help small businesses: "Rarely are you closing a sale. Instead, you are opening the door to the next step." Whatever the goal is, follow through.

Know the Subject

Do you know your topic well enough to describe it in a single sentence? It's harder than it sounds. As Mark Twain pointed out, "I didn't have time to write you a short letter, so I wrote you a long one." Knowing your subject well also gives you the ability to stand out from others who might be doing something similar. The issue, as always, is less what you do, and more what you can do for somebody. "I'm a real estate agent" is not as

Have Two—or Ten—Minutes?

Elevator pitches can also form the building blocks of longer presentations. Milo O. Frank, author of *How to Get Your Point Across in 30 Seconds or Less*, suggests looking at each of the points in an extended presentation as individual 30-second messages. "During the two, three, five, or ten minutes that your speech lasts, you'll have an opportunity to ask—and answer—several provocative questions, paint more than one picture, use more than one personal anecdote or experience. The strategies that kept your listener alert and interested in your 30-second message will achieve the same effect in a longer speech," says Frank.

powerful as saying "I am a real estate agent who specializes in helping first-time buyers like you buy great homes in this town."

Know the Audience

"The worst pitches come from those who don't know my organization or how we operate. Pitching me on something that just isn't possible wastes both my time and theirs," says Yancey. Before going to a conference, he identifies and does research on the individuals he wants to meet. Then he tailors his elevator pitch to match his audience's requirements. "If people don't hear a benefit for them, they won't listen to you," says Yancey.

Organize the Pitch

"Some people are blessed with charisma and persuasiveness," says Dave Power, a marketing partner at Charles River Ventures, a venture capital firm in Waltham, Mass. "We all aren't that lucky. But you can still be very effective by focusing on what is meaningful. You have to organize the flow of information to make it as easy as possible for the brain to digest." Typically, elevator pitches start with an introduction, move into a description of the problem, outline potential benefits for the listener, and conclude with a request for permission to proceed to the next step in the relationship.

Hook Them from the Opening

You have to make an immediate connection with the audience. This connection signals that it's worth investing valuable time to hear what you have to say. Weiss suggests starting with a provocative, contrarian, or counterintuitive statement that will rev pulses. One example: "Quality doesn't matter."

Plug into the Connection

Once you have the attention of your audience, deliver your message. Clarity is more powerful than jargon. Use analogies the audience can relate to. Power once had to explain a new technology called "strong authentication."

He held up an ATM card. "Every time you use this card with a PIN code, you are using strong authentication," he said. The audience instantly understood that strong authentication involved multiple levels of security. Personalize your message by relating your solution to audience needs. Emotional appeals are also powerful.

Presentation Matters

It's natural to want to speak at an auctioneer's tempo. But rapid-fire delivery rarely conveys confidence and command. In fact, a timely pause is an effective attention-getter. "It gives emphasis to what you're saying. It gives you time to think. It gives your listener an opportunity to hear, absorb, and retain what you're saying," writes Frank.

Incorporate Feedback

Use videotape to evaluate your own performance. Give the pitch to someone unfamiliar with your project. If she gets lost in jargon or fails to see the potential benefit, chances are that your target audience will stumble, too.

The benefits of elevator pitches extend beyond persuading your audience. They can help focus your thinking and writing. They can ultimately increase your productivity, allowing you to communicate your message to more people.

Should You Use a Teleprompter?

Teleprompters used to be out of reach for all except national politicians and CEOs. Now they're virtually standard equipment in business meetings of any size or importance. Should you use one?

An accurate answer requires that you be honest about your abilities behind a podium. If you're a nervous speaker for whom presenting is a continuous nightmare from the moment the date is set to the moment you say "thank you" and step down from the stage, then a teleprompter can be a highly useful crutch. It almost always makes weak speakers a little better. It brings your eyes up from off the page, and forces you to move your head from left to right with some regularity as you scan the two text images in front of you. Since the teleprompter screens are transparent, the audience gets the impression that you're looking at the crowd.

The downside of using a teleprompter, however, is that reading text creates a barrier between speaker and audience. Few people can read with all the life and passion that they converse. And a teleprompter traps you behind the podium. Unless you're a politician at a rally, with supporters looking for reasons to leap to their feet

Employees shouldn't stumble when asked, "what does your company do?" or "how can we help?" An effective elevator pitch can outline win-win objectives, and establish a launch pad for a deeper relationship—converting a chance meeting into an opportunity.

and scream their enthusiasm, it's very difficult to connect with an audience in a visceral way when you read from behind the podium.

So it's your call. If you're a confident speaker, you're better off without one—unless you're accepting your party's nomination for president. If you decide to use one, here are a few tips to make the experience better:

1. **Rehearse.** Reading a teleprompter is not a natural human activity. Give yourself some time before the day itself to practice and get used to it.
2. **Learn from President Reagan.** Reagan varied the pace with which he rotated his head, thus giving the impression that he was looking at the audience spontaneously.
3. **Vary your pace and pitch.** Don't fall into a monotone, unvarying rhythm as you read. Speed up. Slow down.
4. **Be ready with a backup.** Occasionally the teleprompter breaks down—it happened to President Clinton during a State of the Union address. Keep a printed text on the podium and keep your place in it.

—Nick Morgan

For Further Reading

How to Get Your Point Across in 30 Seconds or Less by Milo O. Frank (1990, Pocket Books)

Reprint C0201E

Are You Asking the Right Questions?

• • •

John Baldoni

Asking questions, as simple an act as it may seem, can constitute a surprisingly subtle and effective management strategy. And like any other strategy, there is an art to it. While attorneys use leading questions to bludgeon witnesses on the stand for information, playing Perry Mason in the business world is unlikely to yield the desired results.

In fact, it's almost certain to yield just the opposite: It may encourage employees to hide information for fear of not having the right answer. It also encourages employees to shield bad news from their bosses—a communications recipe for disaster.

But at the right time, in the right meeting, the right question can be a powerful tool to help managers explore, discover, and illuminate—and help their employees achieve new levels of productivity.

Why You Need to Ask Them

"Genuine inquiry, or asking questions to elicit the thinking and questioning of another person, is fundamental to learning. Through inquiry, a manager not only learns from employees but also facilitates the learning of employees by stimulating self-reflection," says Stephen J. Gill, an organizational learning and human performance consultant based in Ann Arbor, Mich. Questions are "not about testing employees to hear if they have the right answers," he says. They're "about helping an employee think more deeply about their actions and the team's actions to improve future performance."

People in positions of authority need to ask questions for other reasons.

"One of the great traps of power is the way in which persons on top find themselves surrounded by a bubble of reassurance. It does not matter how accessible or easygoing bosses think they are: No one wants to deliver bad news," says Eliot A. Cohen, professor and director of strategic studies at Johns Hopkins University. "In that and in other ways—the natural effects of pressure, responsibility, and vanity—leaders lose that sense of reality, which so distinguished someone like Lincoln." Cohen profiles Lincoln, along with other wartime civilian leaders in his new book, *Supreme Command* (Free Press, 2002). "The art of questioning is, in other words, essential simply to know what is going on in an organization and its environment."

How to Ask Them

The most effective way for a manager to ask questions is in a collaborative atmosphere, so that she's telling the employee, in essence: "Tell me what you know so we can work together." Managers also need to make it safe for their people to ask questions.

> There is a lot in common between good leadership and good teaching.

Don Winkler, former CEO of both Bank One Finance and Ford Financial, believes in creating "a mechanism that permits fully integrated communication. I call it a family meeting. Family meetings are stakeholder gatherings in which the way is cleared to achieve your vision, purpose, and strategic objective." At a family meeting, people have the freedom to raise questions that in ordinary circumstances might be perceived as threatening to management. For example, employees are encouraged to ask questions about why things are done, how they are done, and what impact they have on the people involved. This can only occur if you put boss and employee on the same level.

"Putting people first will lay the groundwork for creating and sustaining breakthroughs," says Winkler. "We examine what is working and what isn't, in a way that promotes candor, responsibility, and teamwork. In family meetings there is no room for blame."

What to Ask When

Below we take you through the various stages of a project, describing the questions you need to ask at each stage.

Get the Lay of the Land

Managers first need to know what's going on in the trenches. So start every regular or staff meeting with a line of questioning about what's uppermost in employees' minds now. Likewise, close the meeting with "Any new business? Any questions?" so that you don't leave things unsaid or undone.

The key is to ask the questions both at beginning and end as neutrally as possible. If you lead too much at these points, you'll unconsciously close out lines of questioning by hinting to your employees what you want to hear.

Map Out the Purpose

If you've developed a good sense of what's out there, you're ready to move on to the purpose of the meeting. Michael E. Porter, Harvard Business School professor and author of definitive texts on strategy, has said, "The essence of strategy is choosing what not to do." So as well as asking, "What should we do?" ask, "What don't we—or won't we—do?" For example, when it comes to delivering value to the customer, companies need to define what value means and doesn't mean for them—is it performance, is it durability, is it price, or is it all of the above?

Plan Like the Marines

Once the project has moved into the planning stage, use a tool the U.S. Marines use for their missions: SWOT analysis. Ask about Strengths, Weaknesses, Opportunities, and Threats.

Raise Expectations

Once the basic structure of your action plan is clear, it's time to raise everyone's sights. Questions can be used here to get people to aspire to what might have seemed impossible. Ask what your people can do, but also push them to consider stretching.

Challenge the Status Quo

Once the project is under way, you need to rock the boat once in a while during those regular project meetings. Too much time in the comfort zone leads to complacency. During the Second World War, Winston Churchill was famous for asking questions that changed assumptions about the battlefield. He used questions strategically to challenge assumptions and get his generals thinking about alternatives.

Diagnose the Difficulty

When things go wrong, as they inevitably will, try root-cause analysis. Ask a series of "Why?" questions to uncover the cause of a problem rather than its symptoms. Keep asking until you run out of possibilities. It's a useful tool for working to the heart of a difficulty.

Change the Mission

Sometimes when dealing with roadblocks or seeming dead ends, a question can change the vision and mission of an enterprise. Don Winkler believes in the "power question," which he defines as a question "that by its asking leads to a breakthrough in one's thinking."

"Often a power question questions something that has previously been taken for granted," Winkler explains. The answers, he says, will enable people to prioritize, change processes, and improve business results. A power question such as "Who is our customer?" can lead managers to focus on what adds value, such as product selection and customer service, rather than on internal processes that diminish value by forcing employees to look away from the customer.

Ensure Follow-Up

After the meeting is over, don't let yourself get out of the loop. Managers who continue their questioning will avoid surprises and keep employees from growing complacent. Follow-up questioning is a particularly good tool for managers who are new to their employees because it lets them know the manager cares about details and it keeps them on their toes. If an employee doesn't know the answer to a question on the spot, ask her to find the answer and report back at a given time. Do this not to embarrass her, but rather to ensure that things are getting done.

Encourage Dissent at All Times

The best-laid plans are those that can withstand the most serious questions throughout the life of the program. The U.S. military encourages junior officers to challenge plans developed by higher-ups. Citing the concept of "command presence," Cohen says, "Good senior officers can encourage their juniors to ask questions, but they do so more by tone and attitude than by any stock phrase."

Some of the questioning occurs in staged settings, such as in after-action reviews, when everyone from the rank of private on up gets a say, but it also takes place in informal settings—around the coffee pot as well as in the field, he says.

Time and again corporate executives who witness these challenges during stays at military training exercises are amazed at the openness of the questioning. But the military has learned the hard way. Better a timely question ruffles the brass than a failed mission harms a squadron of soldiers.

Create a Culture of Learning

Cultivating an atmosphere in which asking questions is not only tolerated but encouraged opens new paths to learning. Stephen Gill advises, "Train other managers to inquire for learning, not to test, penalize, discipline, or castigate."

Gill further encourages managers to learn to ask open-ended questions designed to get the employee thinking about what he has experienced. "What happened? How close was this to what you wanted? What could you have done to get closer to success? What could others have done to help you be successful? What will you do in the future? What have you learned?" In other words, don't take the process of asking questions for granted.

"Be self-conscious about doing it," says Cohen. "Think of questions in terms of categories: Some are informational, others designed to evaluate personality, still others to prompt thought. Think, too, in terms of sequences of questions.

"In this, as in other respects, there is a lot more in common between good leadership and good teaching than one might think."

Reprint C0303C

Is One-Dimensional Communication Limiting Your Leadership?

• • •

Theodore Kinni

The head of the hospital called the meeting. He wanted all employees to understand that the organization had to find new revenue to survive. Throughout his talk, the administrator cited an impressive array of numbers to prove that growth was essential. But later, as employees filed out of the room, one of the nurses was heard to mutter, "Yeah, well, cancer grows, too."

What did that leader do wrong? He had marshaled reams of data; he had his facts cold.

But in his focus on the factual, he neglected the other two channels of leadership communication—the emotional and the symbolic. If you want to lead people, you have to communicate via all three channels, since people receive messages in different ways. Too many people are one-dimensional communicators—and don't realize they aren't getting their messages across.

For instance, in a 2002 survey of 1,104 employees around the country, 86% of the respondents said that their bosses thought they were great communicators. But only 17% said their bosses actually communicated effectively. "We thought there was a communications gap, but it turned out we were totally wrong. It's not a gap; it's a chasm," says Boyd Clarke, who includes the survey in his book *The Leader's Voice: How Your Communication Can Inspire Action and Get Results!* (SelectBooks, 2002).

Clarke and coauthor Ron Crossland studied hundreds of leadership messages in various media to rank the best practices in corporate communication. "When your intent is to move people to action, to help them understand and deepen their appreciation and gain more insight and more passion about their work, you have got to have all three: Facts, emotion, and symbols," says Crossland, vice chairman of tompeterscompany!

This is not to say that all channels have to be used in equal measure. For one thing, there's overlap between the emotional and symbolic channels, because symbols are shorthand ways of conveying both emotion and meaning. And for another, facts—particularly financial data that may have been hidden from employees before—have enormous power.

But relying on facts alone, despite their power, is a doomed strategy. When a leader communicates via only one channel, the receiver is forced to make sense of the information by filling in the blanks on his own—and the meaning that the receiver creates is often not what the communicator intended. The lesson, says Clarke, is that "adding the other two channels in the appropriate ways at the appropriate times dramatically increases the chance of the communication getting through."

Here are some ways you can maximize the power of your communications by ensuring that you use all three channels.

Don't Recite the Facts—Interpret Them

"In business, we worship at the altar of data," says Crossland. But the factual channel "is not about data; it's about interpretation."

This highlights a common communication disconnect: Managers recite the data instead of interpreting it. "People don't want a recitation," Crossland says. "What they want to know is, What sense do you make out of this data? What is the conclusion? Do you have a logical flow in your thought process? And can we see that?"

Use Emotion to Amplify Communication

"I was a numbers-only guy," says Dave Browne, CEO of Family Christian Stores, a 325-store religious products retailer (Grand Rapids, Mich.). "Absolutely. My background initially was 'Let the facts drive decisions.'"

The numbers had served Browne well. At age 30, he became CEO at LensCrafters, a growing optical retail chain founded in 1983 on the concept of one-stop, one-hour eyeglasses. And that was when Browne realized the facts were standing in his way.

"On their own, facts are capable of delivering one level of results," he says. "But they are also detrimental in terms of holding you back from a higher level of results." To lead the company to those higher levels, the young CEO needed to "communicate on a much higher plane, emotionally and with vision," he says.

After he recognized his problem, Browne decided to start an offsite meeting with 100 key executives by apologizing for his narrow, bottom-line-only focus. "I told them I was not happy, and that I had a pretty good sense I was making quite a few of them unhappy," he says. "I said I wanted to spend more time looking at ways to add value to lives, where to add value to the customer experience, and to act more like a true servant leader than a manager."

Browne tapped into what Clarke and Crossland define as the emotional channel of the leader's voice. There are two components to this channel. The first, the communicator's ability to genuinely and appropriately share his emotions, is one that many business leaders find uncomfortable. "It was frightening," says Browne, "because the picture I had of a CEO is that there was not a whole lot of vulnerability. And when you start sharing dreams and fears and talking about things at an emotional level you are risking vulnerability. But it's worth it."

> Effective leaders use three channels to make sure their messages get through.

Storytelling is an important tool for leaders who want to connect on an emotional level, Clarke says. "Personal stories tell followers what the leader feels and why they feel that way."

The second component of the emotional channel is connecting with constituents' emotions. "Imagine a CEO standing up and saying, 'Our goal is 32% increased profits for next year,'" says Clarke. And he gives the strategies to get there. Some people in the audience are excited, some are angry, and at least a few are frightened. If a leader can speak to those emotional threads in ways that show that he understands and genuinely cares, then this wall that is so easily built up between constituents and leaders starts to crumble, he says.

How to Mix Your Messages for Maximum Impact

Make a story around the numbers. Make sure each piece of data fleshes out the story and supports a conclusion.

Use metaphors and analogies. A gigabyte can be described as the size of one thousand novels; an acre is about the same size as a football field.

Display data visually, but don't get carried away. Go easy on color and other glitzy effects, include titles that make the point clear, and keep the display simple enough to be understood by a high school student.

Put facts in context. The fact that the power of a computer chip roughly doubles every 18 months is not very informative to a listener who doesn't understand the implications and benefits of a more powerful chip.

Want to add symbols to your communication, but don't know where to start? "Invite an advertising person and a marketing person to lunch and tell them what you are trying to communicate and brainstorm with them," suggests Clarke. "That is a lot of what they do all day."

Leverage the Power of Symbols

Symbols are powerful because they fuse emotion and logic into a sort of communications shortcut that employees see and instantly understand. Take the case of Turner Network Television (TNT).

"For twelve years, TNT had not been branded. It had been what is called a 'general entertainment network' where anything could go," says Steve Koonin, the network's executive vice president and general manager. Launched in 1988 to capitalize on Ted Turner's purchase of the MGM/UA film library, TNT had gained a solid audience by delivering a varied mix of programming. The problem was that by 2000, over 200 competing channels had emerged, and TNT, which didn't stand for any one entertainment segment, had a tough time differentiating itself with viewers.

Koonin, a senior marketing executive at Coca-Cola, was hired to create the network's first-ever strategic brand positioning. With his help, the network decided that TNT would become the channel to turn to for drama.

But before he could sell the "We Know Drama" brand to viewers and advertisers, Koonin needed to sell it internally. For a brand to be successful, he says, employees have to live it. "We had to do more than just say this is what we are now and put a logo on a board. Because if you don't live it and you don't believe it, you won't be it."

For instance, TNT's internal version of television's Emmy Awards, the Annual Drammy Awards, are now a fixture at the network. The first Most Dramatic Meeting Award went to a pregnant vice president whose water broke in a staff meeting.

In an eye-opening symbol of management's commitment to the new brand that made a huge impact among employees, Koonin approved the cancellation of the top-rated program in all of basic cable, TNT's *WCW*

Monday Nitro, because professional wrestling did not fit the new brand.

The results of TNT's branding initiative were dramatic. The reprogrammed network was rolled out to the public in June 2001. By the end of the year and again in 2002, TNT was ranked first among basic cable channels in delivery of adults, aged 18–49 and 25–54, in prime time.

"There are a thousand ways to communicate symbolically," adds Clarke. "There are ceremonies and awards and logos. There are drawings and designs and mementos. Metaphors can be very powerful symbols. Songs and poems and jokes and quotes, all of these things can be very good symbolic communication."

Reprint C0305A

Using Nonverbal Communication

. . .

Nonverbal communication—facial expressions, gestures, body language, actions—conveys as much information as the spoken word during a face-to-face encounter. The components of nonverbal communication are legion, and experts differ on what various behaviors signify. However, the most effective communicators carefully control the messages they convey through nonverbal means—and learn how to interpret others' nonverbal signals.

The selections in this part of the volume examine the impact of thoughtful listening; dispel long-standing myths about smiling, touching, and other nonverbal behaviors; explain how to convey energy and confidence through body posture; and show you how to influence others through your own facial expressions as well as how to interpret others' expressions.

How to Listen

Listening Is an Integral Part of
Good Business Communication

• • •

Richard Bierck

Among the many reasons why companies fail, there is one that managers rarely recognize: the failure to listen.

Failing to listen to what your clients want wastes their time, much to the pleasure of your competitors. Failure to listen to your colleagues is equally pernicious. When communication breaks down between managers, finger-pointing ensues and relations deteriorate. The malaise of not listening can be contagious: poor listening by managers can set a bad example for employees, leading to a corporate culture of aural indifference.

Listening requires discipline. You need to rearrange some mental furniture to make room for a conversation, and for the information and nuance it will bring. This means making time.

Of course, setting aside time assumes that you have time to set aside. Managers lacking in effective time management skills often don't. "The most overlooked reason for poor listening is poor time management," says Bill Brooks of The Brooks Group, a sales training and consulting firm based in Greensboro, N.C. "People don't take the time to receive the message."

> ## "The most common reason for poor listening is poor time management."

Many who don't open their receptors are caught in what is known as the activity trap. That's what it's called when people overwhelmed with work fail to set priorities and begin dispatching tasks, in no particular order, to make themselves feel better. If someone calls or comes into their office to discuss a future project of great importance, the immediate tasks at hand, however trivial, may keep them from paying attention. Moreover, Brooks says, the stress that comes from poor time management means that "people will listen mainly to their

00
3 How to Listen

own voice"—the one that's complaining inwardly of unaccomplished tasks.

Once the mind is freed to listen to others, there comes another challenge: listening in a way that suits your particular mental wiring. This can make a significant difference in how much of a conversation or meeting you comprehend and retain.

Cognitive research has shown that individuals process auditory information differently. There's a spectrum of processing styles, running from the strongly linear to the strongly associative. "Linear" listeners take in material as it's presented, effortlessly following the speaker from point A to point B. "Associative" listeners are wired differently. They tend to connect the ideas presented to things they already know. Though they don't tend to follow the speaker step by step, they are nonetheless able to comprehend the material.

Truly linear types are capable of listening passively. They don't need to take any special measures to enhance their listening, for it comes naturally. "Strong auditory processors sit and focus," says Frank Sopper, president of OptiMind Training & Consulting, a firm in Putney, Vt., that helps executives improve their ability to think and learn. "Their faces are like radar screens; they're drinking in your every word."

By contrast, many associative types aren't effective listeners when they're this passive; they must do something. If they're text oriented, they may increase their attentiveness by taking notes. Others listen better if they

7

can restate what they've heard. Or they may do better by asking probing questions. "Thinking of questions helps them be sure of what they're hearing," says Sopper. "It helps them test the limits of their understanding."

Within the linear-associative spectrum, some people rely on body language to fill in the blanks. As there's no way to read body language on the telephone, these people naturally "listen" better to face-to-face conversations.

Then there are people whose attention tends to wander when they sit down. "When I sit down, I lose focus; I'm a movement person," says Sopper. "This kind of person might want to tell the speaker that they listen better while standing."

Regardless of what type of listener you are, there are some things you can do to improve your attentiveness beyond merely adapting to your capabilities.

Set the scene for attentive listening. Avoid having serious conversations in your office, where a loaded desk, a ringing telephone, and an insistent e-mail program compete for your attention. That's what conference rooms are for. Or consider the great outdoors. More and more, managers are taking walks on corporate campuses to give colleagues the attention they deserve—and get some exercise in the process.

Get to meetings early, if only by a few minutes. This interval provides a mental transition zone between stress of travel and the state of mind necessary to concentrate on the meeting. "People need time to compose themselves," says Michael Kemp, a senior consultant at

GoAmerica, a national wireless service provider based in Hackensack, N.J. "Ask yourself: Are you ready to be there? What is your purpose for being there? What outcome do you want?" This self-assessment makes for better listening.

In conversation, be aware of how much talking you do compared with the other person. If the conversation is lopsided, this may tell you something about your listening skills.

Resolve not to let your mind wander. However, don't risk further inattention by berating yourself when it does. If you're prone to drift because of something the speaker says, make a quick note to come back to your thoughts later. This makes it easier to resume paying attention.

Listening is only part of the listener's role. The other part is to demonstrate that he is paying attention. Many speakers who don't think they're being listened to have a tendency to cut things short or to shut down altogether, even if they have worthwhile things to say. Appearing attentive involves far more than an occasional "uh-huh." Here are some pointers:

Relax, but not too much. If your body's at rest, it's a sign that your attention may be resting as well.

When there's a long pause, be aware that the speaker may be waiting for feedback. This is a good time to ask clarifying questions. Keep them short, then say, "please continue." More in-depth questions can come after the person is finished speaking.

The Idea Bank

www.idea-bank.com

It's not unusual for professional speechwriters to refer to dozens of reference books or comb the Internet looking for material, but the typical businessperson doesn't have time to sift through a large amount of information when preparing a speech. Charles Francis's site, IdeaBank, makes it simple to find material related to your topic.

Francis, a former senior communications executive with IBM, has gathered material such as jokes, anecdotes, quotations, and proverbs on a wide range of topics. What sets IdeaBank apart from similar sites, however, is the keyword search function. Each item in the database has from 5 to 15 keywords attached to it. The keyword itself does not have to be in the quotation in order for it to come up in your search. For example,

Be aware of whether you might be what Kemp amusingly calls "an appeaser"—someone who nods in agreement, or even makes insincere comments such as "Is that right?" though they're not listening to a word. Such individuals may come from families with nagging parents, and they need to unload this psychological baggage before they can become effective listeners.

Give cues that are genuinely encouraging, even when there may be disagreement. When there is strident disagreement, people tend to listen only to their own linked to key words such as "bureaucracy," "democ-racy," "substance abuse," and "self-discipline."

Another feature of this site is the History File. Simply enter a month and day, and the IdeaBank will display a number of historical events that happened on that day, as well as a list of notables who share that birthday.

It's also worthwhile to click on the "Speech Tips" icon on the main page. This series of brief essays offers advice on how to effectively use anecdotes, historical data, and humor in your speeches.

IdeaBank is a fee-based service targeted to communi-cations professionals, but a large number of its sub-scribers are business executives. The site offers a free trial period during which you can download up to 100 items over a 30-day period, whichever comes first. If you decide to continue with the service, you can choose a subscription plan based on the number of items you think you'll download.

points—and if they're not heard, to make them over again in the same ineffectual manner. To give the speaker the cue that you are indeed listening even if you disagree, acknowledge their point. One way to do this is to say: "What I understand you to say is. . . ."

When you're aware of the subject of an interchange in advance, try to identify your biases and put them in abeyance. This way, they're not as apt to show in your facial expressions, and the speaker is more apt to fully convey his or her points.

Above all, if you feel yourself slipping away, don't be afraid to ask the speaker to go over the point you missed. Skilled speakers are usually able to tell from that glazed look in your eye, and they'll only lose respect for you if you feign attentiveness. This will save time, money, and something more valuable: the speaker's respect.

Reprint C0101B

The Truth Behind the Smile and Other Myths

Reading Body Language Is Important,
but the Clues May Be Misleading

• • •

Nick Morgan

Most people call it "body language"—the clues to the meaning and intent of communication from others that we get from gesture, facial expression, posture—everything that isn't spoken. The experts call it "nonverbal communication," but it amounts to the same thing: a second source of human communication that is often more reliable or essential to understanding what is really going on than the words themselves.

Or is it? Accurate knowledge of body language is essential for success in interpersonal relations, whether in the business world or in personal life. However, much of our understanding is instinctive—and a good deal of it is wrong, according to modern communications research. What follows are some of the hardier myths, and the reality behind them.

Eight Myths and the Reality

1. A liar can't look you straight in the eye

There is a persistent belief that people with shifty eyes are probably lying. As Paul Ekman says in his classic work, *Telling Lies: Clues to Deceit in the Marketplace, Politics, and Marriage,* "When we asked people how they would tell if someone were lying, squirming and shifty eyes were the winners. [But] clues that everyone knows about, that involve behavior that can be readily inhibited, won't be very reliable if the stakes are high and the liar does not want to be caught."

Ekman goes on to argue against attributing too much meaning to such behavior for two reasons. First of all, although this kind of nonverbal communication most reliably signals the presence of some kind of emotion, that emotion may or may not mean that someone is lying. Nervousness can, for example, manifest itself as shifty eyes. But there are many reasons for nervousness. To understand what the behavior means, you still have to interpret the emotion.

Second, Ekman has found that one group in particular excels at making eye contact that appears very sincere: pathological liars. Hence, it is not safe to rely on eye contact as a measure of sincerity or truthfulness.

2. When meeting someone, the more eye contact, the better

This long-held belief is the inverse of the idea that shifty-eyed people are liars. The result is an unfortunate tendency for people making initial contact—as in a job interview, for example—to stare fixedly at the other human. This behavior is just as likely to make the interviewer uncomfortable as not. Most of us are comfortable with eye contact lasting a few seconds, but any eye contact that persists longer than that can make us nervous. We assume that there is something else going on—an attempt to initiate flirtatious behavior, perhaps. Indeed, studies on flirting show that prolonged eye contact is an early step in the process.

3. Putting your hands behind your back is a power gesture

For years presentation coaches have taught people to put their hands behind their backs in what is sometimes called the "Prince Charles" stance, in the mistaken belief that the heir to the British throne is a good model for strong body language. Since he's a prince, the thinking goes, and he stands that way a lot, it must be powerful.

> Body language conveys important but unreliable clues about the intent of the communicator.

Actually, the research shows that most people find the gesture untrustworthy—if we can't see what your hands are doing, we're suspicious. So if your goal is to increase trust in any given situation, don't put your hands behind your back.

4. "Steepling" your fingers shows that you're intellectual

Again, this technique is one that has been taught by many speech coaches. A good deal of research over the years correlates hand gestures toward the lower part of the face with thinking—stroking the chin, propping the chin in the hand, putting a finger on the cheek. If thinking is a sign of intellectualism, we should presumably be demonstrating this trait by indulging in a lot of hand-to-face contact.

The experts distinguish between "emblems," which are gestures with specific meanings in certain cultures, and gestures, which are intended to assist meaning but lack specific content. An example of an emblem is the hand sign that indicates "OK" in the United States. The same emblem has an obscene meaning in some Mediterranean countries.

An example of a gesture is the waving of hands we all indulge in when searching for a word. Steepling falls somewhere in between; it is a gesture without any specific meaning, but it is more deliberate than a mere waving of the hands. The best that can be said about it is that it may signal intellectual pretensions on the part of the communicator!

5. High-status people demonstrate their dominance of others by touching them

Another widely accepted belief is that powerful people in society—often men—show their dominance over others by touching them in a variety of ways. In fact, the research shows that in almost all cases, lower-status people initiate touch. And women initiate touch more often than men do.

In his book *The Right Touch: Understanding and Using the Language of Physical Contact,* Stanley E. Jones describes a study of a public health organization: "The group studied was a detoxification clinic, a place where alcoholism is treated. This was an ideal setting in which to study status, sex roles, and touching. . . . [The] findings showed two clear trends. First, women on the average initiated more touches to men than vice versa. Second, touching tended to flow upwards, not downwards, in the hierarchy."

6. People smile when they're happy

People smile for all sorts of reasons, only one of which is to signal happiness. Ekman describes many kinds of smiles, from the "felt" or true smile to the fear smile, the contempt smile, the dampened smile, the miserable smile, and a number of others. Daniel McNeill, author of *The Face: A Natural History,* says, "Smiling is innate and appears in infants almost from birth. . . . The first smiles appear two to twelve hours after birth and seem void of content. Infants simply issue them, and they help parents bond. We respond; they don't know what they're doing. The second phase of smiling begins sometime between the fifth week and fourth month. It is the 'social smile,' in which the infant smiles while fixing its gaze on a person's face."

Whatever their origin or motivation, smiles have a powerful effect on us humans. As McNeill points out, "Though courtroom judges are equally likely to find smilers and nonsmilers guilty, they give smilers lighter penalties, a phenomenon called the 'smile-leniency effect.'"

7. Voices rise when speakers are angry

Again, nonverbal communication reliably signals the presence of emotion, but not the specific emotion. A rising voice is associated with a variety of emotions, including anger, but also nervousness, fear, excitement, hysteria, and others. You must always consider the communicator and the context carefully. Experts like Ekman warn that unless you have a good understanding of someone's basic communication patterns, you will have little hope in accurately deciphering the person's less routine signals.

"The best-documented vocal sign of emotion is pitch," says Ekman. And yet he also says, "While most of us believe that the sound of the voice tells us what emotion a person feels, scientists studying the voice are still not certain."

8. You can't trust a fast-talking salesman

The belief that speed and deception go together is a widespread and enduring one. From the rapid patter of Professor Hill in *The Music Man* to the absurdly fast speech of the FedEx guy in the TV commercial from a few years back, we react strongly—and suspiciously—to fast talk. People talk at an average rate of 125 to 225 words per minute; at the upper end of that range listeners typically find themselves beginning to resist the speaker. However, as Ekman says, the opposite is greater cause for suspicion. Speech that is slow, because it is laced with pauses, is a more reliable indicator of deception than the opposite.

"The most common vocal deception clues are pauses," says Ekman. "The pauses may be too long or too frequent. Hesitating at the start of a speaking turn, particularly if the hesitation occurs when someone is responding to a question, may arouse suspicion. So may shorter pauses during the course of speaking if they occur often enough. Speech errors may also be a deception clue. These include nonwords, such as 'ah,' 'aaa,' and 'uhh'; repetitions, such as 'I, I, I mean I really . . .'; and partial words, such as 'I rea-really liked it.'

"These vocal clues to deceit—speech errors and pauses—can occur for two related reasons. The liar may not have worked out her line ahead of time. If she did not expect to lie, or if she was prepared to lie but didn't anticipate a particular question, she may hesitate or make speech errors. But these can also occur when the line is well prepared. High detection apprehension may cause the prepared liar to stumble or forget her line."

Most of the research into nonverbal communications shows that people are not very good at masking their feelings. Emotions do leak out regularly, in many ways. And yet, the research also shows that most of us are not as good at decoding those emotions as we would like to think. Young people are significantly worse at both signaling emotions and reading them. Although we do learn as we grow older, we should remain wary; in the end, body language conveys important but unreliable clues about the intent of the communicator. The more information you can get about the clues you are trying to decode, the more likely you will be to decode them correctly.

For Further Reading

Telling Lies: Clues to Deceit in the Marketplace, Politics, and Marriage by Paul Ekman (2001, W.W. Norton & Company)

The Right Touch: Understanding and Using the Language of Physical Contact by Stanley E. Jones (1994, Hampton Press)

The Face: A Natural History by Daniel McNeill (2000, Back Bay Books)

Reprint C0208A

Are You Standing in the Way of Your Own Success?

● ● ●

Nick Morgan

The way you stand could change your life. Immediately. For businesspeople, stance is an important indicator of how deeply you are engaged with your job, how much you believe in the products you are selling, how confident you are that your company will survive.

And that's just for starters. Did you know that you are likely to make or break a sale by what you do in the first fifteen seconds after entering the customer's office—before you say anything? Or that you can increase your attractiveness to others—and your success in your career—by how you move your head? Or that the seat you take at a table will determine, in part, the direction a negotiation will take?

These insights and many more are at the heart of modern communications research, and *Teach Yourself Body Language*, by Gordon Wainright (McGraw-Hill, 2003), summarizes much of it in very practical terms that readers can put to work immediately to change their lives.

Take stance. Wainwright suggests an experiment in which you stand straight, tuck your tummy in, hold your head high, and smile at those you meet. Do this for a week, concentrating especially on those who normally don't seem to be very friendly in your workplace. Wainwright predicts, based on many such experiments, that you'll find people treat you differently immediately. You'll garner more respect, you'll be taken more seriously, and you'll find that even the grumpy ones warm up to you.

Your stance, broadly speaking, signals to the world how energetic, confident, and powerful you are. Slumped shoulders, a downcast gaze, a slow pace, and a sagging belly are taken by the world to mean that you lack confidence, that you don't have much energy, and that you are probably less important, successful, and powerful as a result. These impressions may be neither accurate nor fair, but they are the inevitable results of the fleeting impressions we tend to get of one another during the course of a busy day.

Those are just the fleeting impressions. Stance and what used to be called your bearing can play much more important roles when you're negotiating an important contract or trying to close a sale. We like to deal with winners, and we are more inclined to yield negotiating points to people who appear to be operating from a position of strength.

And what about those first 15 seconds after entering a room? Wainwright reports research that measured the status of people who enter an office. Low-status people tend to linger at the door. Medium-status people go in halfway. And high-status people go in all the way to the desk and sit down next to the occupant.

To increase your attractiveness, Wainwright suggests 10 categories of behavior to monitor and improve. Studies show that attractive people tend to be more successful, everything else being equal, so more than mere likability is at stake here.

The 10 categories are:

1. EYE CONTACT: The more the better, up to visual intrusiveness.

2. FACIAL EXPRESSION: Be lively, smile a lot, look interested.

3. HEAD MOVEMENTS: Nod to show interest, keep your chin up.

4. GESTURES: Be expressive and open, without overdoing it.

5. **POSTURE:** Stand erect, lean forward to show interest, lean back to be informal.

6. **PROXIMITY AND ORIENTATION:** Get as close as you can to people without crowding.

7. **BODILY CONTACT:** Touch as often as you can without causing offense.

8. **APPEARANCE AND PHYSIQUE:** Go for color in dress, fitness in physique.

9. **TIMING AND SYNCHRONIZATION:** Speed up your activities to just before the point of inefficiency.

10. **NONVERBAL ASPECTS OF SPEECH:** Try to balance your need to talk with the need to listen.

If taking on all of these desiderata sounds like a tall order, take heart in the knowledge that doing even a few of them will begin to increase your attractiveness to others. You don't have to manage them all at once. In fact, you don't have to manage them at all, if you can find enthusiasm for your job, your colleagues, and your activities in general. If you are enthusiastic, you'll discover that you'll naturally increase your attractiveness by unconsciously doing many of the behaviors on the list.

Reprint C0306D

What Your Face Reveals and Conceals

Eight Communication Lessons
from the Research Front

* * *

Does the face contain the window to the soul—or is it a mask? We spend a great deal of time every day attempting both to show and to conceal how we feel about the events swirling around us. Much of that emotional display takes place in the face. We also expend a great deal of effort trying to decode what others are showing and concealing with their faces.

In business, our careers can thrive or wither depending on how good we are at this game. Daniel Goleman's work on "emotional intelligence" has amply demonstrated the link between ability to understand how others are feeling and success at the highest reaches of the business world. No matter how expert you are at your job, argues Goleman, if you don't develop the skill of understanding others' emotional lives, you will never climb to the top of the greasy pole of success.

The face is the best place to begin. From infancy, we follow faces more avidly than anything else. One study found that babies began to recognize their mothers' faces more than 50% of the time after only 1.7 days. This interest sticks with us throughout our lives, but most of the knowledge we gain is unconscious.

Lessons on the Unspoken Language of the Face

1. It Pays to Be Good Looking

A good deal of the research on facial communication corroborates common sense, but some of the more surprising findings turn our cultural assumptions upside down. For starters, one study showed that babies look at attractive adult faces longer than plain ones. Sadly, we never become much more sophisticated in our looking.

This bias toward the merely pretty extends throughout life. Judges are not more likely to find ugly people guilty, but they do give good-looking people easier sentences. Attractive people earn more than plain ones in comparable jobs and rise higher in their careers. It literally pays to be good looking.

2. To Increase Your Appeal, Blink Less

Of course, you can't easily change your physiognomy. But, oddly enough, research on blinking suggests some strategies to increase your attractiveness to others. Contrary to folk wisdom, blinking is not necessarily a sign of guilt or nervousness. It is an indication that the mind of the blinker has wandered to something else. We blink more when we talk than when we listen, and in fact use blinking to control the ebb and flow of conversation. One researcher, for instance, argues that we blink in order to signal that we wish to interrupt. Actor Michael Caine was so convinced of the importance of blinks that he painfully trained himself not to blink at all in order to increase the power of his close-ups (when his eyes might be 20 feet across on the wide screen) and to decrease the likelihood that the director would cut away from him to some other actor. As Caine realized, people like to be paid attention to—and not blinking at them increases their sense that you care about them and are therefore attractive to them. There's more to eye contact than conveying sincerity, in other words. It also affects how other people rate you for attentiveness—and thus attractiveness.

3. Women Are more Facially Expressive than Men

The research does confirm one folk wisdom, that there are facial differences between men and women. Some are familiar, some unexpected. Surprisingly, men's faces are more mobile than women's, but that effect covers only minor muscle movements. Women's facial muscles are, on average, smaller, so that small motions and twitches of the face don't show up as readily. But overall, women are more facially expressive. They report themselves as feeling stronger emotions than men and are more accurate in matching facial expressions with the emotions they are expressing. The business implication? Men may need to work harder to express emotions in their faces—and read others' facial gestures—if they are going to succeed at the upper levels of the business world.

4. Looks Do Deceive—but We All Make the Same Mistakes

People of all cultures respond similarly to certain facial features. We all imagine that high foreheads are a sign of intelligence, for example, though research has shown they are not. We equate facial signs of aging—retreating hairlines, smaller eyes, and broader faces—with dominance, even though there is no necessary connection. We also equate signs of anger—lowered brows and narrowed eyes—with power and authority. Large eyes and high eyebrows, on the other hand, convey kindness and warmth to us. None of these connections have a factual basis.

But advertisers use babyfaced spokespeople to generate trust and older-looking faces to generate authority because they know what most people believe to be true.

5. The Face Has a Basic Repertoire of Emotions— Learn Them

Universally, people recognize a basic group of emotions. Researchers differ on precisely how many, but there is fundamental agreement on enjoyment, anger, fear, surprise, disgust, and sadness. Perhaps not surprisingly, these correspond to the basic movements of the eyes, eyebrows, and mouth. We widen the eyes to show interest, narrow them to show negative emotions like anger and disgust (when combined with other facial gestures). We raise the eyebrows to show surprise and interest, lower them to show anger and sadness. We smile and frown, raising and lowering the mouth to show good and bad feeling.

This is the basic repertoire of the face, and it is understood around the world. To be effective communicators, we need both to know these expressions well in others and to use them clearly in our own communications. And it takes practice. Aside from skilled actors, most people are not very good at manipulating these basic expressions to conceal their feelings. But here's a good place to start: the most important technique for determining sincerity and truth (and their opposites) in our colleagues, teammates, competitors, business partners, customers, suppliers, and the rest is to listen and

Why We Never Forget a Face

When we're being attentive, do we really know who we're looking at? Research has shown that we are extraordinarily good at recognizing individual faces, even when we've glimpsed them only briefly. How do we accomplish this feat? Researchers at the MIT Media Lab determined that we recognize patterns in parts of faces, which they call "eigenfaces." By dividing the face up into about 20 eigenfaces, reliable face identification is possible. The system is being used to develop face recognition software that is proving to be the most accurate and economic system for individual identification yet created. From these beginnings, developing computers and other everyday machines that respond to our individual faces will be relatively easy. Imagine a car, for instance, that starts itself when you sit down in the driver's seat and smile at the rearview mirror!

watch for a match between the words and the facial expressions.

6. Real Facial Expressions Are Fleeting

For example, genuine expressions of anger and surprise are quite fleeting. They last for a second or two at most. One sign of insincerity, then, may be an expression that lingers on the face for a longer period of time. In general, the onset of a genuine expression matches quite precisely the beginning of the feeling. So watch out for expressions that come seconds later than other signals of the emotion in question, such as the words that voice it.

When, for example, facing a business opponent in a negotiation, who appears to have a real "poker face," watch the eyes. Very few people are able to control the widening and narrowing of the eyes and pupils that go along with signs of pleasure and displeasure, anger, and happiness. The muscles around the mouth may not move, but the eyes cannot hold still for long.

7. Don't Stare

And the eyes are the most important part of the face. For instance, we are extraordinarily sensitive to staring. We don't like being stared at, and when we can't avoid it, we try to escape. Researchers (with a streak of cruelty) stood on street corners and stared at drivers stopped at traffic lights. The drivers accelerated on green faster than those the researchers ignored. Similarly, stared-at pedestrians walked away faster than those left alone. Students in college libraries who are stared at leave earlier, on average, than others not so persecuted. You can use this insight to help make colleagues more comfortable (by not staring) or, in situations where the opposite is appropriate, more uncomfortable.

8. Make Yourself More Attractive

When we are attracted to someone else, it is the eyes that attract us first. Widened eyes and pupils in response are a sign that the interest is mutual. After that, researchers have identified the following universal attributes of beauty:

Wide cheekbones	Narrow cheeks
Broad smile	Wide nostrils
Wide eyes	High-placed eyes
Eyes set far apart	Large pupils
High eyebrows	Small nose

What is interesting about this list is how much of it we can control. We tend to think of beauty as something we're born with or not, but in fact much of beauty is behavior—and makeup. Physically, we can widen our smile, our nostrils, and our eyes and raise our eyebrows. Makeup can effect changes in all the other areas—and while the use of makeup has been traditionally confined to women and actors, that is slowly changing.

Our faces are the most important signs we put forward to the world to show who we are and what we care about. It is up to us to decide what that face should be and what it should reveal. It is both a window to the soul *and* a mask. We control both its momentary expressions and its destiny.

For Further Reading

Matthew Turk and Alex Pentland, "Eigenfaces for Recognition," *Journal of Cognitive Neuroscience*, Vol. 3, No. 1, 1991, pp. 71–86.

What the Face Reveals edited by Paul Ekman and Erika Rosenberg (1998, Oxford University Press, 495 pp.)

Nonverbal Communication in Human Interaction by Mark L. Knapp and Judith A. Hall (1996, Harcourt Brace, 512 pp.)

The Face by Daniel McNeill (1998, Little, Brown and Company, 288 pp.)

Primal Leadership by Daniel Goleman, Richard Boyrtzis, and Annie McKee (2002, HBS Press, 336 pp.)

Reprint C0006D

"Reading" Others' Signals

· · ·

Skillful face-to-face communicators not only control the spoken and nonverbal messages they're sending; they also work diligently to interpret others' messages as accurately as possible. By studying your audience—particularly the emotions your listeners are experiencing and the spoken and nonverbal cues they're sending—you can boost your chances of dissolving resistance and bringing opponents over to your side. You can also improve the likelihood that you'll detect falsehood in others. Finally, you can determine others' personality types (extravert? introvert?) and learn to speak their "language"—increasing the chances of more effective face-to-face exchanges.

Get Around Resistance and Win Over the Other Side

• • •

Liz Simpson

It's budget time again. You're sitting across from the head of R&D, and once again the two of you are at odds. Money's being cut yet again, and it's come down to this: Either your study of that new Asian market gets funded, or it gets cut, and leading the charge to cut it is Mr. R&D. Why is he always against whatever you put forward? It's not like he has a better idea for how to spend the money. He just seems to want to kill your project. What can you say to him to change the game?

You recognize the situation all too well; many a persuasion opportunity you face today in your job probably feels much the same. You're confronting people across the table whose heels are already dug in, holding onto a position that is virtually opposite your own. You talk, they talk, and nobody moves. Whether it's a sales opportunity, or a new product you like and they don't, or an argument over a budget—minds seem to be already made up. How can you turn the stalemate into a chance to move the opposition around to your point of view?

Experts on motivation and persuasion offer proven steps you can take to make your attempts in this difficult game more successful. The first and most important step is to take a close look at your audience.

Study Your Audience

"Many of us assume that to be persuasive all we have to do is spend our time and energy making people understand what it is we're saying, so our preparation goes into the content of the message. What's really needed is the willingness to consider, first and foremost, your audience," says Rick Maurer, an Arlington, Va.–based management consultant who has advised organizations including Lockheed Martin, IBM, and AOL Time Warner on achieving employee buy-in on change-management initiatives.

To succeed at the persuasion game, you have to be absolutely committed to understanding the other side's position as well as your own. Without that willingness to try on the other side's arguments, you simply cannot be persuasive. From that understanding will come the insights you need to move the other side over to your camp.

Maybe Mr. R&D sees all marketing studies as a waste of time because his interest lies in creating new products. Perhaps you could recast the study in terms of its allowing a new idea to reach fruition.

"Peter Drucker once said something to the effect of 'Communication takes place in the mind of the listener, not the speaker.' Your goal as a successful communicator is to relate everything you say to what is already known inside that listener's mind," says Anne Miller, a New York City–based communications coach. "You need to understand that each of us is a collection of our own memories and experiences, and it's through them that we know the world, develop our perceptions, and filter all new information that comes into our minds and hearts. The best communicators understand this fact and break down resistance by using analogies and metaphors to reach common understanding and acceptance."

Pay Attention to the Emotion

Understanding your audience means understanding their resistance to your message, the *Why* behind their *No*. Overcoming resistance by looking at it in terms of three intertwined levels your audience may be operating on, rather than taking a single overarching approach, is the cornerstone of Rick Maurer's book *Why Don't You Want What I Want? How to Win Support for Your Ideas Without Hard Sell, Manipulation or Power Plays.* The essence of two of the three levels is emotional.

Which leads to another key point: Pay attention to the emotion your opponent is experiencing. That's basic to understanding, but it's something that businesspeople shy away from because emotions are messy and often awkward to deal with.

Maurer explains that what he calls Level One resistance relates to the content of your idea and is concerned with disagreement over how your message is being interpreted, illustrated by the other party saying, "I don't get it."

Level Two and Level Three resistance, however, spring from emotion. Level Two resistance almost always originates in the fear that the other party feels as a consequence of your idea, manifested by their saying, "I don't like it." An example of Level Two resistance is how employees react when an executive announces that a major restructuring may result in some downsizing: They don't like the idea because they're afraid they might lose their jobs.

The most challenging type of resistance to overcome is Level Three resistance, in which the other party is not objecting to your idea but instead to you or to what you represent. The message here is "I don't like you."

While each objection you face may involve more than one of these resistance levels, if you're to have any chance at all of winning others around, then it's the emotional content of Level Three that should be your principal focus. "Failure to treat Level Three resistance as real and legitimate is a key reason why many people fail to turn opposition into support," says Maurer.

How does Mr. R&D really feel about you and other marketers? Understanding these emotions, even if they're not pleasant, is the key to getting started on bridging the differences.

Listen Up

To see things from another's point of view and to build trust with her, you have to listen closely to what she says. Only then will you have a chance to persuade her to see things from your perspective.

"If you think listening is not critical, just think how you feel during a lunch date when the other person talks the entire time about his or her concerns, interests, products, or services," says Miller. "Your most immediate thought is, When can I reasonably call for the check? There's an old sales saying: 'God gave you two ears and one mouth. She must have wanted you to listen twice as much as she wanted you to talk.' If you don't listen to the other side, you will never break down their resistance or win them to your point of view."

This is the approach that Chippewa Falls, Wisc.–based communication professional Lin Grensing-Pophal has taken throughout her 20-year career in health care, energy, and education, during which she's seen others make the mistake of trying to establish credibility and gain the upper hand by dominating the conversation.

"Before you can be persuasive, you have to give people a reason to believe and trust you. Only then will it be much more likely that others will try to 'get' your message and try to like it, because they like you," she says. "It's a bad professional move to try to effect change without taking the time to listen to the views of others. That's why I always recommend finding out as much as you can about the background players and where each of them stands on a particular issue."

Determine What Kind of Learner You're Dealing With

As you listen to your opponent, take note of how he best receives information. Only then can you present your case in the most effective way.

While working as a political intern during his college years, Tim Heffernan—now an account director with the public relations company KCSA (New York City)— learned to overcome resistance to his messages by listening to others' choice of vocabulary. "There are three different ways that people learn: Auditory, visual, and kinesethetic," says Heffernan. "The clue to a person's dominant style is illustrated by their use of phrases like 'I hear you,' 'I see what you're saying,' or 'I feel . . . .' When someone uses a lot of auditory references, I'll frame something similarly in response, such as: 'It sounds to me like. . . .' By tuning into their dominant style, I'm much more likely to overcome the problem of their not hearing what I have to say just because they process information differently."

Make Your Verbal and Nonverbal Messages Consistent

In this difficult game of persuasion, you not only have to understand how your listeners will best hear the information you're giving them, but you also have to present that information in highly consistent ways. In other words, your nonverbal communication has to be consistent with your verbal message. For example, you will fail to persuade someone if you telegraph with your body language that you're holding a weak hand, despite what you're saying.

Children as young as four or five can be highly persuasive, according to research conducted by Colgate University psychology professor Caroline Keating, who, like Heffernan, defines persuasion as the verbal and nonverbal art of manipulation. She found that the children who exerted the greatest influence over their groups were also highly skilled at deception. The same was true for adults.

"We discovered that individuals who got their way in group situations were also highly persuasive when telling a deceptive story, such as drinking something very bitter and unpleasant and convincing us, on camera, that in fact it tasted good," says Keating.

So does this mean that when developing persuasion skills we also need to learn how to lie convincingly?

"We weren't interested in our subjects' ability to lie but in their acting skills," says Keating. "Remember, though, that we require our leaders to lie all the time, in looking confident when they're anxious, or appearing refreshed when they're dog-tired. That may be why they're leaders, because they can control and inspire us through their nonverbal behaviors."

> If you haven't thought about overcoming interpersonal resistance by monitoring your nonverbal behaviors, you should.

Keating recalls a recent interview situation in which an otherwise excellent job candidate—who was saying all the right things—undermined himself in nonverbal ways. "He had his back turned toward one of the panel and I predicted that was the person who would give him his lowest rating. Then, when one of the interviewers said something really dumb, this guy responded by leaning back in his chair and dropping his smile. Doing that was a disaster and I predicted—again, accurately—there would be his second-lowest grade."

Already there were two people around the table who weren't listening at all because of the candidate's nonverbal behavior. What can undermine your efforts most of all, points out Keating, is that these cues are so subtle they often operate under the cognitive radar screen and thus people don't even know why they don't like you.

Essentially, she says, if you haven't thought about overcoming interpersonal resistance by monitoring your nonverbal behaviors, you should; you need to rehearse them as much as what you're going to say.

Present Their Point of View
Before Your Own

The final secret to persuasion is to present your opponents' point of view before your own when you know the subject is contentious.

"If you're wading into an audience you know is already biased against you and is highly informed about the issue," advises Keating, "then you're best presenting a two-sided argument—theirs and yours. Doing that robs them of the opportunity to resist you; they have to participate in the solution. One thing I know from studying people is that getting someone to help make the rules means they're more likely to play by them."

Taking other people's perspectives into account requires considerable thought and practice. But the effort pays off, particularly in environments where building and maintaining long-term relationships is considered more valuable than realizing short-term gains. This is increasingly the case in organizations that rely on internal and external strategic alliances where parties may have similar goals but different ideas about how to achieve them.

If long-term cooperation is important to you, it's crucial to develop techniques that can help you win support for your message without a bruising battle.

For Further Reading

MindControlMarketing.com: How Everyday People Are Using Forbidden Mond Control Psychology and Ruthless Military Tactics to Make Millions Online by Mark Joyner (2002, Steel Icarus)

Why Don't You Want What I Want? How to Win Support for Your Ideas Without Hard Sell, Manipulation, or Power Plays by Rick Maurer (2002, Bard Press)

Reprint C0304A

How Can You Tell When Your Teammate Is Lying?

Revealing the Hidden Clues to Deceit

• • •

How can you spot a liar? Paul Ekman, one of the world's experts on this subject, tells us that it is both harder and easier than you might think. His classic book, *Telling Lies: Clues to Deceit in the Marketplace, Politics, and Marriage,* reveals both aspects of the ancient game of deceit.

Spotting a liar is hard because most of the standard clues we have come to associate with liars and lying don't, in fact, offer much help. Shifty eyes may only indi-

107

cate nervousness or shyness. People who look us straight in the eyes may be psychopathic—or may simply have convinced themselves of the truth of their own lies first. And in the end, you may just want to believe the lie. Hitler was able to convince Chamberlain that he wasn't about to invade Czechoslovakia in part, according to Ekman, because Chamberlain wanted so much to believe him.

But for those who want to be able to detect truth from fiction, Ekman offers some tips to make it easier. He begins by telling us flat out that "there is no sign of deceit itself—no gesture, facial expression, or muscle twitch that in and of itself means that a person is lying." There are, however, signs that betray emotions that are at odds with the story the person is telling us.

Liars typically put most of their focus on the words they utter. Thus, while the first place to look for the lie is in the inconsistencies of a story, the liar may have his story pat. But that is only the first line of defense, says Ekman. He notes that clues to lying may be found in so-called Freudian slips and other stumbles of the tongue. If someone on your team says, "I don't love that idea—I mean I do love it," consider the possibility that she may in fact have told the truth in the first phrase. A Freudian slip is more likely to reveal negative emotions, which are harder for us to express in the happy-talk culture of business.

What are the best signs of lying? Ekman counsels us to look for what he calls leakage—in the voice and in the body. Leakage occurs when the liar betrays her nervousness or guilt with a gesture or change in voice timbre.

For example, the two main verbal clues are easy to spot. Ekman's research shows that people pause more, and commit more speech errors, when they are lying than when they are not. Furthermore, their voices tend to rise in pitch—a sign of stress.

Of course, to spot these clues, you have to know what the person sounds like when he is not lying. Ekman emphasizes that it is almost impossible to spot a lie in someone whose behavior you're not familiar with. Thus, you'll have more luck spotting liars among the teammates that you know well, rather than among, say, a group of negotiators from a big supplier that you are meeting for the first time.

From the body come two kinds of clues. One is the "emblem," or gesture that has a specific meaning in a particular culture. For example, Ekman relates the story of the student who inadvertently revealed her true feelings about being interrogated by her professor. As the interview grew more adversarial, the student raised her middle finger in the classic gesture. Her hand was placed in her lap at the time, and neither she nor the professor were consciously aware of it. Similarly, the shrug, especially if half-completed, is another useful sign of emotion at variance with the surface story. Keep an eye out in particular for symbolic gestures that take place out of the normal display range of such expression, which is between the waist and the neck. A coworker who scratches his face with an upraised middle finger, for example, may be signaling concealed anger.

Another group of gestures has no specific meaning; Ekman calls them "illustrators." These are the hand wavings we all indulge in as we speak. We do more of these when we are agitated, and increased illustrating may be a sign of deception. If a normally reserved colleague suddenly begins to gesture excessively, look out for deception or concealed emotion.

Finally, the trickiest clue comes from the face itself. By videotaping liars and replaying their facial expressions in slow motion, Ekman has proved that people betray emotions contrary to the ones they are trying to convey with "micro-expressions": fleeting frowns that betray the smile, expressions of disgust that betray the fixed look of happiness, and the like. It takes training to be able to spot these micro-expressions, but it's possible with practice. The smile is a particularly revealing example. True smiles light up the eyes and the mouth, and create wrinkle lines around the corners of the eyes. Smiles composed of a mixture of emotions tend to involve only the mouth, and they may sometimes have the corners turned down. Keep in mind that such a smile may indicate not a lie, but simply less-than-heartfelt pleasure.

Armed with Ekman's insights, we can become more adept at spotting liars in everyday life—or become better liars ourselves.

For Further Reading

Telling Lies: Clues to Deceit in the Marketplace, Politics, and Marriage by Paul Ekman (1992, W.W. Norton, 366 pp.)

Reprint C0001E

How to
Speedread People

* * *

Instead of the enthusiasm you hoped for, you're getting questions. You called the meeting to get the team charged up about the new software demo, but you're getting quibbles back. "Exactly how long does it take to train people to use this thing?" "Why is the opening page in inverse colors?" "Won't that confuse customers rather than help them?" You're thinking, all these questions are about irrelevant details! You just wanted to get the team to start thinking! Why are they bogged down in implementation? This is just a demo, for heaven's sake!

You leave the meeting frustrated and confused. You thought you had a good team. It's done great work in the past. What's going on?

Scenes like this one are repeated daily in offices around the world. The root problem is the different ways people have of learning, listening, and reacting to new ideas. We tend to treat people in ways that make sense to us, but that may not make sense to other personality types. Figuring out how to adjust your communication style to suit the varieties of personality will save headaches and effort and make for a more efficient workplace.

One time-tested approach to figuring out how people differ is the Myers-Briggs Type Indicator, a simple personality test that places people along four continua: extraversion-introversion; sensing-intuition; thinking-feeling; and judging-perceiving. While grouping personalities in broad types always runs the danger of over-simplification, the Myers-Briggs categories have proven surprisingly robust over the years. Many businesses routinely test their employees to see how well they fit together under this schema. But the difficulty has been knowing what to do about the differences once they're identified. And, of course, you can't take the time to test everyone you meet.

Enter Paul Tieger and Barbara Barron-Tieger. In their book, *The Art of Speedreading People*, they give valuable tips on how to quickly estimate which personality type you're dealing with on that sales call or in that business meeting with folks from another division. Then they offer suggestions on how to communicate more effectively with those types.

Personality Types

Extraverts vs. Introverts

Extraverts immediately impress you with their energy. Filled with animation, they tend to be quite physical, waving their hands around to make points, and displaying lots of emotional range. Introverts, on the other hand, are restrained physically, and project calm and reserve. In groups, especially, extraverts gain energy, whereas introverts may withdraw. An extravert may well seek to be the "life of the party"; introverts rarely do. Extraverts may dress more flamboyantly than introverts, who are comfortable in quieter clothing.

In communicating, extraverts usually talk more and louder than introverts. Introverts talk less, and focus less on the people they're talking to. Introverts are likely to use the word "I," where an extravert would say "we." Extraverts often talk faster than their introvert counterparts, and they move more rapidly from one topic to another, whereas introverts like to explore single topics in depth.

How to Tell the Sensor from the Intuitive

According to Tieger and Barron-Tieger, about 65% of the U.S. population are "sensing," whereas only 35% are intuitives. So the odds are two to one that the person you're meeting is a sensor.

That said, you still need to be able to tell the difference. Try the apple test. If you hand a sensor an apple, and ask her to describe it, you'll get something like the following: "It's a McIntosh apple. It's round, and smooth, with a few brown spots. It's cool in my hand. It feels ripe. It's about the size of a baseball."

An intuitive, on the other hand, might say something like this: "Apples. They started the whole thing—in the Garden of Eden, I mean. You can use them for pies, applesauce, cobblers, apple juice, and a host of other things. You can give one to the teacher. An apple a day keeps the doctor away, so they must be good for you."

The intuitive is reporting just as honestly as the sensor, but she is telling you her feelings and associations, whereas a sensor gives you specific facts. Sensors tend to speak in short phrases, where intuitives ramble more. Language for an intuitive is a plaything. For a sensor, it is a tool. Sensors like physical or slapstick humor best, while intuitives like more cerebral forms of humor. Intuitives tend to finish others' sentences, whereas sensors are more likely to wait until others have completed their whole thought. Intuitives repeat and recap; sensors are typically direct and to the point.

Sensors are more aware of their bodies, on the whole, and thus are more naturally graceful. Natural athletes tend to be sensors. Intuitives have a long track record of bumping into things. Sensors have a greater tendency to dress fashionably, and appropriately to the activity, while intuitives may dress to suit themselves.

The Differences Between Thinkers and Feelers

This type is relatively easy. Men are likely to be thinkers—some 65% of the male population fits this type. Women, on the other hand, are the reverse: some 65% are feelers. But don't assume too much, or you'll leave out the other 35% of each population.

Thinkers are cool where feelers are warm in interpersonal relations. Feelers will go out of their way to help people; when you're likely to say of someone, "He [or she] is just nice," that person is liable to be a feeler. Feelers are more ready to reveal personal information about themselves, and more ready to share feelings. A feeler is likely to put much more energy into choosing just the right gift or card. They are more often sentimental, and less fond of violence in movies or on TV.

Thinkers, on the other hand, are assertive and tend to appear more confident. They like to get to the point quickly, with a minimum of time wasted. Where feelers shun conflict, thinkers are more likely to insist on having it out. But feelers will get very upset if their deepest values are threatened. Thinkers are less likely to take things personally. Feelers are often easily hurt.

In communicating, feelers tend to be good at finding areas of agreement, where thinkers are better at precisely delineating areas of difference. Where feelers are emotional, thinkers are factual. If you ask a thinker how he or she feels about something, you'll typically get an argument about what the word means. A feeler, on the other hand, will be happy to oblige you with a complete answer.

Judger vs. Perceiver

Judgers outnumber perceivers by about 60% to 40%. In demeanor, judgers appear more formal, whereas perceivers are more casual. Where judgers are restrained, serious, no-nonsense, perceivers are more fun-loving, playful, or irreverent. Judgers like to be in charge; perceivers are ready to "go with the flow."

Judgers often appear to be in a hurry. Perceivers are more apt to give the appearance of calm. They may, in fact, be less organized than judgers; they may not be in a hurry because of having forgotten they were supposed to be somewhere. Judgers are typically better able to manage their time. Judgers are more likely to be properly dressed, where perceivers will be as casual as the occasion allows. Hair can also provide a clue: someone who looks like he is having a perpetual bad hair day is liable to be a perceiver.

In communicating, judgers appear decisive and deliberate. Perceivers may have a harder time making decisions. In giving opinions, judgers tend to be forthright and assertive, where perceivers may appear more flexible and less determined to take one particular course of action. In work styles, judgers place emphasis on the product. They like to get one project done before starting on another. Perceivers, on the other hand, favor process over product, and they are more easily distracted. Where judgers like structure, rules, and clear procedures, perceivers are much more comfortable with ambiguity.

How to Communicate with Each Type

Talking to Them in Their Own Language

So once you've learned how to recognize the various types on the fly, what do you do about it? One way to apply these insights is to shape your communications in ways that make it easier for various types to "hear" you. Once you speak the "language" of other types, you'll find that meetings will become more productive and you'll be able to get your own points across more successfully.

Talking to Extraverts and Introverts

Once you've identified an extravert, you can experience greater communications success with her, first of all, by communicating verbally rather than in writing. Let her talk and think out loud. In a meeting, provide a variety of topics so that the extraverts can stay engaged. Keep the meeting moving along; don't belabor certain issues. Strive to get immediate action out of the meeting.

If you know you're dealing with an introvert, on the other hand, spend more time listening than talking. Take on one subject at a time. Write, rather than talk; introverts feel more comfortable in the cooler medium of print rather than the hurly-burly of face to face. Allow time for reflection and consideration. If you do meet with them in person, don't finish their sentences.

Communicating with Sensors and Intuitives

Sensors like clear delineation of the topic at hand. Have a strong case ready; offer facts, examples, cases. Present your information in a step-by-step fashion, and make it practical. Speak in complete sentences. Make it real: use lots of past examples to buttress your arguments.

Intuitives, on the other hand, prefer to get a sense of the big picture first. Why are we here? What are the implications? What are the possibilities? Use analogies and metaphors, and go light on the facts—and the details. Be ready to brainstorm options, and figure out ways to engage them on the imaginative level. Let them figure out the possibilities in the ideas you are presenting.

What to Say to Thinkers and Feelers

With thinkers, be organized and logical. Make sure you've thought through the logic flow of your presentation or discussion. Does cause come before effect? Does what you're saying make sense? What are the consequences of your proposal? Don't ask them what they "feel"; ask them instead what they "think." Appeal to their sense of decency, fairness, and propriety. Be concise; don't repeat yourself.

Feelers, on the other hand, will appreciate it if you begin with the points of agreement you already have. Make sure you acknowledge their contributions in language that shows you understand and respect their emotions. Address the "people" issues; don't focus solely on the facts of the business. Maintain good eye contact, and smile frequently. Be friendly.

Succeeding with Judgers and Perceivers

When you call a meeting with a judger, show up on time and ready to go. Have a clear agenda, and cover all the points. Resolve the issues you bring up; and draw appropriate conclusions. Find ways to be decisive. Better yet, let them make decisions. Be efficient; don't waste their time or yours. Have a plan, and stick to it.

With perceivers, be ready to depart from the agenda. They will have lots of questions; respect their need to ask. Don't force decisions on them; better to allow them to make the decision after the meeting. Allow for a lengthy discussion of options, opportunities, direction changes, and mid-course corrections. Pay attention to the process, not the product. Give them choices. Work to incorporate their contributions into the flow of the discussion.

Putting It All Together

While the process is by no means foolproof, paying attention to the clues that others give you in everyday workplace interactions will allow you to form quick impressions of their personality types. By using different communications styles for different types, you'll have a better chance of connecting with people in ways that make it easier for them—and more successful for you. They'll be more likely to understand your point of view, and be more favorably disposed toward it. Not all business scenarios lend themselves to resolution just because the communication is effective among the parties present, but poor communication certainly can derail an otherwise promising deal. Use these four continua of types to improve your communication style and eliminate unnecessary static in the give-and-take among your business colleagues.

For Further Reading

The Art of Speedreading People: Harness the Power of Personality Type and Create What You Want in Business and in Life by Paul D. Tieger and Barbara Barron-Tieger (1999, Little, Brown and Co., 224 pp.)

What Type Am I? Discover Who You Really Are by Renee Baron (1998, Penguin USA, 208 pp.)

Reprint C9904A

Communicating Under Pressure

• • •

When face-to-face encounters occur between people who are highly stressed, under great pressure to obtain one another's support, or angry, the opportunities for misunderstanding proliferate. For that reason, you need a special set of techniques for communicating under these conditions. The articles in this section provide suggestions for managing your own stress so that you communicate more effectively, as well as handling notoriously difficult situations—performance reviews and other encounters that spark anger or defensiveness in employees, circumstances in which you need to exert influence on others over whom you have no formal authority, and the delivery of valuable critical feedback to coworkers.

Don't Let Stress Strain Communication

• • •

Anne Field

Stress is endemic to the workplace today. The declining stock market, layoffs, weak earnings reports, corporate scandals—they've all contributed to an atmosphere of grim uncertainty and intense pressure as fewer people do more work in a tougher competitive climate. One of the most potentially troublesome results of stress for managers is what it can do to your ability to communicate—and to others' ability to communicate with you. Just when you need to be operating at utmost efficiency, stress can complicate and distort communication in a variety of ways, making it even harder to perform effectively.

125

Thus taking steps to address stress should be your top priority, even if you have 20 items on your to-do list. You have to devote serious attention to communicating, "even though you'd probably much rather be concentrating on getting things done," says Bobbie Little, director of executive coaching for the Center for Executive Options, a division of DBM, the New York–based career transition and outplacement firm. "But, you'll ultimately be more effective than you would if you were to ignore the problem."

Of course, a certain amount of stress is a natural part of life. In fact, some stress can be a productivity booster, pushing us to work harder. It's when people are under too much stress that the trouble starts and their ability to communicate is impaired. Some of these problems include:

Trouble concentrating. As the body prepares to handle a perceived threat, the stress hormone cortisol shuts down the neurons in the brain, preventing it from being able to store new information, says Marcia Reynolds, author of *How to Outsmart Your Brain* (Covisioning, 2001).

Result: you have a harder time paying attention. That means your employees will have difficulty taking direction and understanding your wishes when they feel uncertain or threatened, regardless of the source. And, you, too, will find it tougher to listen and follow through effectively.

Unclear directions. You have a million things to get done and fewer staff members to help you do them.

So, without realizing it, you take shortcuts—for example, you give shorter, quicker, less clear explanations and directions. The result, of course, is that your staff doesn't understand what you want. Feeling under pressure themselves, they hesitate to ask for more clarification. What happens then is that "the work that comes back isn't what you expected," says Diana Sullivan, senior vice president of strategy and services for the leadership development/coaching division of Lee Hecht Harrison in San Francisco.

> Under intense pressure, your communication style may change, thoroughly confusing your staff.

Defensiveness. With their defenses worn down, your employees may react more irrationally than they might under calmer conditions. A neutral comment may be interpreted as a criticism and unnecessary disagreements and arguments may result.

Forgetfulness. Since your brain is overloaded, your short-term memory can become impaired. As you focus on trying to retain critical information, you may more easily forget what you heard—and what you said.

Distortions in communication style. Under stress, your communication style can shift into hyperdrive. If yours naturally is a logical, linear approach, requiring lots of information, you may find yourself fixating on the need for detail, driving your staff crazy and hurting productivity. But the opposite phenomenon may occur instead. Under intense pressure, your style may change, perhaps becoming very emotional and thoroughly confusing your staff.

How to Avoid Problems

While stress creates a fertile environment for communication disasters, they don't have to happen. Avoiding these potential problems requires conscientious effort, but it can be done. Here are nine key steps to take.

1. Keep Messages Short and Clear

Since people under stress are likely to have trouble concentrating on—and remembering—what you say, it's best to relay thoughts, directions, and information in brief chunks. "Making too many points when the listener isn't capable of taking it all in will be counterproductive," says Mark Gorkin, a clinical social worker and organizational consultant in Washington, D.C., who specializes in stress reduction. After offering one or two points, ask the listener to paraphrase what you just said, to make sure he or she understood. Similarly, if you're listening to someone else, summarize your take on the conversation.

2. Vary How You Communicate and Repeat the Message

People have certain built-in preferences for how they receive information. When you send an e-mail, for example, present your thoughts in various ways so as to increase the likelihood that they'll reach everyone. For big thinkers who look at the headlines and tend to skip over details, include a few headlines; for linear communicators, who tend to read messages methodically from beginning to end, include as many key details as possible.

At the same time, don't just rely on one mode of communication. Since you can count on the fact that some people won't hear you the first time, follow up in a different way. If, for example, you tell someone something in person, back it up with an e-mail or, if appropriate, voice mail.

3. Be Especially Careful with E-mail Correspondence

"When people are stressed out, e-mail is the worst way to communicate," says Paul A. Argenti, professor of management and corporate communication at Dartmouth College's Tuck School of Business (Hanover, N.H.).

Communication in face-to-face meetings and in phone conversations is influenced by nonverbal cues, which are absent in online communication. With e-mail, says Argenti, "you're more likely to say things you'll feel sorry for later." Wait a moment before sending your messages and always read them over first.

4. Encourage People to Ask Questions

If you don't invite your staff to follow up when you're not clear, you're creating a recipe for disaster. Since it's likely that, under pressure, you will unknowingly fail to make your instructions clear, your employees must have permission to pin you down—without fearing they'll appear stupid or irritate you.

5. Take Special Steps with Virtual Teams

Online relationships are hard to read at any time, but they are especially so in a stressful environment. That's because you can't rely on nonverbal signals to know if someone is reacting negatively to stress. As a result, you'll have to be a lot more assertive in your communications—ask probing questions and pick up the phone and call more often than you would otherwise.

6. Look Out for Employees Who Withdraw

Under stress, some people retreat. As a result, they may wind up failing to convey important information, hurting the vital flow of communication even more. Your task: conduct more one-on-one conversations and regular meetings, so it's harder for staff members to remain isolated.

7. Understand Your Communication Style

At no time is this more important than when you're under stress. If you understand your own style, you can begin to evaluate the impact of your behavior on people who work for you. What's more, if you let your employees in on the news, you'll help them learn strategies for working with you under those conditions.

Say you're usually calm and sociable, but become irrational under pressure. Your employees can develop different ways to deal with you, depending on the situation. They'll also understand that your reaction has little to do with their performance and everything to do with your stress levels. At the same time, you can learn to recognize the red flags that tell you if you're about to lose it, so you can take a quick break and get ahold of yourself.

8. Use "I", not "You"

To cut down on the tendency for conversations to become irrational, or for people to take things too personally, avoid statements beginning with "you." "The message is invariably one of blame," says Gorkin. Instead, use the more neutral "I."

For example, instead of saying, "You're wrong," say, "I disagree" or "Here's my position on that." (Keep in mind that saying "I think you're wrong" is just a sneaky way of phrasing a "you" statement.)

9. Slow Down

You may have to take conscious steps to slow things down and, though it may be tough, focus on relationships, not just results. "Pay attention to the process," says Lee Hecht Harrison's Sullivan. She recalls the case of the general manager of a financial services company. A consistently top producer, he tended to pay attention to driving the numbers, especially in stressful situations, with little interest in such time-consuming annoyances as interaction, explanation, or making sure his staff felt engaged by their work. Result: several employees left.

Eventually, he worked with Lee Hecht coaches to learn, among other things, how to make meetings less relentlessly numbers-focused and to speak in a more relaxed tone of voice.

Says DBM's Little, "We have to spend more time in conversation. Less task, more talk."

Reprint C0301D

Managing Anger

Learn to Deal with It Effectively

• • •

Richard Bierck

Most of us react with shock to anger in the workplace. Whether it's an unexpected outburst or an explosion that's long overdue, managers are rarely ready for it when it happens. As a result, we often don't handle it well. We smooth things over and tell everyone to get back to work, but we fail to deal with an important issue: the underlying causes of the anger.

But that's a lost opportunity. These angry confrontations can create an opportunity to improve relationships, experts say, if they're handled right. When faced with the wrath of their employees, skilled managers may be able to turn the anger into something positive by addressing the conflicts and redirecting the displaced energy: this is the alchemy of anger management.

How to Deal with Your Own Anger

When you become angry (an emotion that most people experience several times during each working day), experts suggest you should:

Acknowledge the anger. "If we acknowledge and validate the anger, it is much less harmful," says Weisinger. Anger that is "stuffed" tends to come out in other, even less productive ways like sniping, gossiping, or conspiring behind the victim's back.

Manage the symptoms. As you become enraged, your pulse soars, along with your blood pressure and respiration rate. These are unhealthy symptoms when you're stationary, but not when you're more active. Being active helps you focus and mentally travel a safe distance from the anger's source. "Doing something helps you regain a sense of being in control," says Weisinger.

But first, managers need to learn to criticize more constructively so that their employees don't become more defensive and, in turn, angrier. And managers must learn to manage their own anger, both in dealing with employees and dealing with executives who are higher on the corporate food chain.

None of this is easy. Indeed many companies are now placing counselors on contract to help managers resolve workplace hostilities. But managers who can avoid this expensive alternative will stand out. Those who can't tend to stand out in a different way, says Dr. Caryn Gold-

"I clean up my office and pay my bills. This allows me to channel the anger into productive action."

Be pragmatic. "Are you so angry that you're going to quit your job? If not, then consider other actions you can take to feel better about things," says Weisinger. "What's your best course of action to deal with the problem? Then use problem-solving skills to generate your most effective response."

Confide in a friend. Call on a trustworthy friend with good judgment to help you work through your anger. "The wrong friend will merely stir you up, inciting you to rash courses of action," says Goldberg. "They may also tell others in the company about the conflict, which often gets back to that person. Anyone who thinks this is a good way to get a person to change her behavior is dreaming."

berg, a New York City–based psychologist who handles conflict resolution for corporations.

"Human resources people may say that you should address conflicts with them, but once you do, the big 'T' of trouble-maker is hung around your neck."

The ultimate goal for managers and employees alike should be to transform anger into positive action. "The common denominator of any anger situation is: How do you change? What do you do?" says Hendrie Weisinger, a clinical psychologist based in Westport, Conn., who consults for corporations.

The first step is to emotionally immunize yourself against this highly contagious state. "Self-awareness is the key here," says Weisinger. "You have to work hard to maintain your own emotional perspective."

Then, there are ways to keep the anger from escalating. The foremost is, naturally, to avoid responding in kind. In addition:

Lower the person's level of "anger arousal"—that is, the physical manifestations. Quick movements, a raised voice, a quickened pulse—reducing these symptoms of anger actually helps cure the disease. For example, if the angry person is standing or pacing, invite her to sit down. Anger creates thirst, so offer her a drink of water (but not coffee or other drinks containing caffeine—this will only quicken her already heightened pulse).

Hear the person out, and communicate to him nonverbally that you are indeed listening. This means abstaining from interrupting. "If you're tempted to interrupt, just take a deep breath and remind yourself to listen," says Weisinger. It also means being mindful of your body language: maintain eye contact and a posture facing the person to show you are listening.

Show that you've been listening attentively by summarizing the person's thoughts in your own words. If the person seems skeptical that you actually understand them, Weisinger says, "just stay calm and tell her you really want to understand her point of view. Take a deep breath." Find a way to simultaneously channel the anger into constructive energy and reduce its origins by agreeing on things you can both do to resolve the conflict.

The most fertile breeding ground for workplace anger is when managers offer—and employees respond to—criticism. A fundamental part of the problem, says Weisinger, is our culture's aversion to criticism. "It's viewed as being so negative that instead we use the euphemism, 'feedback.' The word has a negative connotation, but it shouldn't."

As Weisinger writes in his book, *The Power of Positive Criticism,* employees and managers alike should learn to "befriend criticism" as an opportunity for insights into ways to improve. Instead, when we hear the word "criticism," we become defensive.

As they enter critical settings together, employee and employer alike are more likely to become angry. Of course, employers have one advantage: They know when these delicate encounters are most likely to occur, for they're the ones who are paid to be critical.

Managers should take advantage of this foreknowledge by preparing themselves emotionally. "Step back from the situation when you're not at work, and write down what it is about your interaction with this person that may be making them angry," says Goldberg. "Write down what you'll say to her and what you think she'll say back to you. This helps to allay fears of what the other person will say."

Once the discussion begins, managers should pay particular attention to their word choice. "People respond much less defensively when the person doing the criticizing uses less threatening language," says Marie Waung, an associate professor of psychology at the University of Michigan—Dearborn. This not only means being positive, it also means paying attention to things that are seemingly superficial, but actually significant, such as the use of pronouns. Says Waung: "Instead of saying 'You shouldn't do this,' you should say, 'People should do this.'"

The performance evaluation is a setting that's particularly prone to anger. There, says Waung, it's especially important to "allow angry employees to speak their piece. This allows them to participate and makes the meeting a setting for problem-solving rather than an attack."

Then managers must think on their feet. "You can use what the employee is saying to modify or bolster your criticism," says Weisinger. "But you have to actually respond to what he says; you can't just repeat your points. By doing this, managers show that they are truly listening, and this lessens the employee's anger."

Above all, managers should be flexible. If the employee has a good point, concede it. Or if there's a point that could go either way, says Goldberg, "fall on your sword a little."

Flexibility involves helping the employee set up a structure for improvement—whether or not this is likely to be successful, says Goldberg. "When an employee blames a poor performance review on a lack of good assignments in which they could show their skills, what assignments could you give them now? The bottom line: How can you both make changes to move things forward? What are you going to do that's different?"

For Further Reading

The Power of Positive Criticism by Hendrie Weisinger (1999, AMACOM)

Reprint C0111B

When the Direct Approach Backfires, Try Indirect Influence

Six Tactics for Getting Your Point Across with Subtlety

· · ·

Martha Craumer

Have you ever felt that you just weren't connecting with a colleague whose support you needed? Ever tried to work with a team that offered resistance and foot-dragging instead of cooperation? Has your feedback had the opposite effect that you intended—or has it gotten no response at all?

Fact is, leadership and management aren't quite as simple as they used to be. Companies are becoming flatter and less hierarchical; we're "commanding" less and collaborating more. And the new networked organization—with its emphasis on outside partnerships and alliances—means working with people in new ways. Add to this the challenge of dealing with a global, culturally diverse workforce and one thing becomes clear: our traditional approach to leadership—forceful, assertive, and direct—isn't always the best option, especially when the people we're trying to influence aren't direct reports.

So What's the Alternative?

When direct or prescriptive methods of communication and management don't work, you may have better luck with a more subtle, indirect approach. In her new book, *The Power of Indirect Influence,* Judith Tingley explains that "indirect influence attempts are planned as intentional by the leader, but viewed as unintentional by the target person." Here are six alternatives to the direct approach.

1. Beat Around the Bush

Although Western cultures tend toward direct methods of communication, other cultures take a very different approach in their business dealings—in fact, the business itself often seems to be an afterthought. Tingley tells of an American man working in Saudi Arabia who learned that getting something done requires an indirect approach. When he needs information from a government office, he drops by and hangs around for an hour or two, drinking tea and chatting. He knows that eventually one of the workers will ask if he needs help with anything. At that point, he'll act surprised, as if he's just remembered, and then state his need, which is promptly and graciously taken care of.

We all know people who seem to succeed at getting others to do things for them without having to ask directly. We usually chalk it up to "charm." But often, it's just a matter of letting go of the agenda and taking the time to be pleasant.

Advocates of indirect influence assert that it's often better to let people figure things out for themselves, come to their own conclusions, and take initiative on their own. A lack of clarity can put more responsibility on the people you hope to influence—and that's not necessarily a bad thing.

2. Talk Less, Listen More

When trying to win people over to our way of thinking, we often spend too much time explaining and convincing and not enough time asking questions, listening, and understanding other points of view.

People are less apt to put up resistance when they feel that you've taken the time to listen to and really understand their issues and concerns. In his best-selling book, *The 7 Habits of Highly Effective People*, Stephen Covey says that the greatest need of human beings—after physical survival—is to be understood, affirmed, validated, and appreciated. He explains that "empathic listening gets inside another person's frame of reference. You look out through it, you see the world the way they see the world, you understand their paradigm, you understand how they feel." It is human nature to want to work with, not against, someone who "gets" us.

It seems paradoxical, but the harder we try to get our point across, the less likely we are to succeed. Think of the people you know who command the most respect, whom others line up in support of. It's often the person who speaks quietly with a few carefully chosen words that show his or her grasp of the issues at hand. Their power comes from thoughtfully listening—not from title or position.

3. Make 'em Like You

Studies consistently show that we'd rather say yes to someone we like—even a stranger—than to someone we don't like. So how can you increase your likability? Some factors, like good looks, are beyond our control. But there are other things you can do to increase rapport. Key among these is to play up similarities. We tend to like people who are like us, who share our background, interests, opinions, taste, style of dress, and so forth. We also like people who like us. Research shows that human beings are suckers for compliments—even insincere flattery.

Another way to heighten feelings of similarity is to copy the communication style, both verbal and nonverbal, of the person you're trying to influence. Tingley calls this technique "modeling and matching." By matching the gestures, body posture, vocal intonations, words, and speaking style of the person you're with, you can quickly build up comfort levels and rapport.

The social bond is another powerful influencer, as shown by the impact that friendship and name-dropping can have. In his book *Influence,* Robert Cialdini discusses the power of the Tupperware party, noting that "the strength of a social bond is twice as likely to determine product purchase as is preference for the product."

4. Make 'em Laugh

Ever wonder why so many speakers open their presentations with a joke? Humor is disarming, it's the great equalizer, and it makes people root for us. It's hard to feel negative when you're laughing—and hard to dislike a person who makes you laugh.

Humor can be a very effective tool. It makes the speaker appear relaxed, approachable, and in control. It promotes relaxation and openness in the listener, which in turn increase receptivity to change, new ideas, and the influence of others. Tingley quotes Ellie Marek, author of *Eating Roses: Bites of Living Humor:* "Messages rejected when said directly are accepted when said with humor."

> Our traditional approach to leadership—forceful, assertive, and direct—isn't always the best option.

Humor can create a common bond that melts resistance and encourages cooperation. But be careful. Inside jokes and cultural allusions can be off-putting to outsiders. And obviously, humor should never be at the expense of the person you're trying to influence—nor should it make light of their issues or concerns. George Simons, an advocate of humor-driven influence, suggests that the safest approach is humor directed at one's self.

5. Use Stories and Metaphors

Stories and metaphors help us put things in context, view the larger picture, and get in touch with our emotions. Because people make connections between a story and their own life experiences, the messages linger and can inspire real change.

"Good managers use stories to convince others of a particular view, to create shared meaning and purpose, to help create a sense of community," says Tingley. For all of these reasons, storytelling can be a powerful tool for indirect influence.

Metaphors also guide our perception of things and of ourselves, whether we're aware of it or not. As an example of how strongly metaphors can affect those around us, Tingley tells the story of Dan, the CEO of an electronics manufacturing company. To maintain quality, Dan required that shift supervisors run through a quality checklist at the beginning of each shift, but compliance was low. When all direct attempts to influence the supervisors failed, Dan took a different approach. A seasoned pilot, he invited each manager to go flying with him in his private plane. The invitations were met with enthusiasm—until Dan added that he would not be running through the routine flight checklist before takeoff. The supervisors got the message loud and clear, and checklist compliance has increased.

6. Do a Favor—Even a Small One

Doing something for someone gives you enormous power and influence over them—just ask any politician. In his book *Influence,* Cialdini discusses the unwritten rule of reciprocity and how it obligates us to repay what another person has given us. This rule is deeply ingrained, not just in our culture, but in every human society around the world. At one time it was integral to our survival, and it survives to this day—stronger than ever.

Cialdini cites a research study involving a group of subjects and a "plant"—a fellow named Joe—who was posing as a fellow subject. There were two control groups. Each member of the first group received a small "favor" from Joe—a Coke that he picked up for them while out of the room. The second group received no favor. Then, Joe told each group he was selling raffle tickets. The subjects who received a Coke from Joe bought twice as many tickets as the subjects who received nothing. The rule overwhelmed all other factors—including whether they even liked Joe or not. The ticket buyers felt an irresistible need to repay him.

Cialdini's research shows that the size of the initial favor makes no difference and has little bearing on the size of the favor we feel obliged to perform in return. In fact, we typically feel the need to repay with a larger favor. But interestingly, despite this uneven quid pro quo, we also seem unable to refuse the favors of others. Says Cialdini, "Although the obligation to repay constitutes the essence of the reciprocity rule, it is the obligation to receive that makes the rule so easy to exploit." So the reciprocity rule is a dual-edged sword. And we as human beings are apparently unable to resist its pull.

Indirect influence is about personal power, not positional power. It's about reacting to others, without falling back on traditional strong-arm tactics and power plays. In our culture, where directness is highly valued, some of the tactics may seem counterintuitive—even manipulative. But good leaders know that while some individuals and situations require a direct approach, others do not respond well to it—they require the subtlety and finesse of indirect influence. The important thing is to have available a wide range of influence tools and to know when to use them for the greatest impact.

For Further Reading

Eating Roses: Bites of Living Humor by Ellie Marek (1998, Decipher Publishing)

Influence: The Psychology of Persuasion by Robert B. Cialdini (1993, Quill)

The Power of Indirect Influence by Judith C. Tingley (2001, AMACOM)

The 7 Habits of Highly Effective People by Stephen R. Covey (1990, Fireside)

Reprint C0106B

Is There Any Good Way to Criticize Your Coworkers?

An Expert Offers a Road Map to Successful Criticism

• • •

"Criticism comes with the job," says Hendrie Weisinger, a consultant who is author of *The Power of Positive Criticism*. It's something we're all uncomfortable with, yet it's extremely important to our continuing growth in our work lives.

We see criticism as negative, painful, and uncomfortable both to give and to receive. We use the euphemism "feedback" to get around the pain. Yet as soon as the feedback turns negative, we see it as criticism, and we're on the defensive. Is there a better way?

Weisinger believes that there is. His advice is to "befriend criticism. Actively solicit [it] from others." You will learn from it.

How do you give others constructive criticism? By developing a strategy. Plan your criticism in advance. Focus on what you want to change in the person you are criticizing and jot down a few notes about what you want to accomplish.

When you actually get to the criticism itself, says Weisinger, be "improvement-oriented." In other words, don't criticize to blame, but to improve. Don't say, "You really screwed up that sales presentation." Rather, try, "Next time, why don't you make sure that you actually ask for the business? That will improve your hit rate with the customers."

Further, you need to protect the other person's self-esteem. Tell him how important he is to the company. Choose your words with care, avoiding negative words and focusing on what you want the person to do differently the next time. Get the recipient involved by asking him what his perception of the event is. Beyond that, ask the recipient to suggest ways in which he can take specific steps toward improvement and success.

Most people criticize, Weisinger points out, with sentences that follow this structure: "Here's what you did that was good; BUT, here's what went wrong." That strategy will elicit defensive behavior, "and you can forget about the power of positive criticism." Instead, structure your critiques like this: "State how the recipient can improve—AND—state the positive things the recipient is already doing." This formula will elicit a positive response and a willingness to try to improve.

Recasting your criticism along these lines will not completely remove the anxiety surrounding the act of criticizing your coworkers, but it will go a long way toward ensuring that you get a positive response.

More of Weisinger's Tips for Positive Criticism

Tell them what you want. Most criticism fails to achieve its aim because the critic fails to be clear about the desired change. Write it down beforehand and make sure you don't forget to say it in the heat of the moment.

Be timing-oriented. Like justice, criticism late is criticism denied. There is a time and a place for all criticism. It's better to criticize in private, but if that will mean delaying the commentary until much later, public criticism may be necessary.

Use questions Socratically. Devise a series of questions that will bring your recipient to the desired insight. Ask, for example, "How do you think the sales division will react to your marketing report?" rather than saying "You should have checked with the sales division for their reaction."

When words don't work, use your actions. Sometimes you have to intervene to make the desired behavior change happen. In that case, be consistent, forceful, and patient. Keep intervening until the behavior changes.

Use your expectations. Make sure you know what they are. Check to see if they're realistic. And communicate them to everyone else. Otherwise they will just be blocks to progress.

Acknowledge that it's subjective. There's no point in denying what everyone knows: most of the time, it is your opinion you're sharing. Be open about it. In the long run, you'll build credibility, not lose it.

Put motivation in your criticisms. If you shape your criticism to include rewards that will come the recipient's way if she does improve, your hit rate will be much higher.

Use their world. Make sure that you put your comments in terms that your listener will understand, not necessarily in terms that are most comfortable for you.

Follow up, follow up, follow up. Sometimes results are slow in coming, and the criticizer gives up. But it's important to stay focused on getting the result you want. And to notice and acknowledge the results when they do occur.

Know your criteria for criticizing. If you don't know what you want, how will anyone else? One of the best ways to get this across is to show people rather than tell them. If you're trying to develop the perfect software package, show your team something that comes close to what you want. And then paint a verbal picture of what it would take to go all the way.

Listen to yourself. During the critique, stay focused on the job at hand. Talk to yourself to keep yourself on task. Don't let emotion divert you from your plan.

Stay cool, calm, and collected. Criticizing is hard work. Don't make it even harder by giving in to the urge to pound the table or shout at your recipient. When the emotional temperature gets raised to the boiling point, all listening stops. The critique has become a show.

For Further Reading

The Power of Positive Criticism by Hendrie Weisinger, Ph.D. (1999, AMACOM, 184 pp.)

Reprint C0003F

About the Contributors

Betty A. Marton is a freelance writer based in New Paltz, NY.

Loren Gary is editor in the Newsletters and Conferences Group at Harvard Business School Publishing.

Nick Wreden is the author of *Fusion Branding: Strategic Branding for the Customer Economy*.

John Baldoni is the author of *Great Communication Secrets of Great Leaders*.

Theodore Kinni is a business writer based in Williamsburg, Va., who has authored or ghostwritten seven books.

Richard Bierck is a freelance financial writer based in Princeton, N.J. His work has appeared in *U.S. News & World Report, Bloomberg Personal Finance,* and *Parade.*

Nick Morgan is a former editor at *Harvard Management Communication Letter.*

Liz Simpson is an Austin-based business writer.

Anne Field is a Pelham, N.Y.-based business writer.

Martha Craumer has worked in marketing communications at CSC Index, Lotus Consulting, and Zefer. She divides her time between Cambridge, Mass., and Sarasota, Fla.

Harvard Business Review Paperback Series

The Harvard Business Review Paperback Series offers the best thinking on cutting-edge management ideas from the world's leading thinkers, researchers, and managers. Designed for leaders who believe in the power of ideas to change business, these books will be useful to managers at all levels of experience, but especially senior executives and general managers. In addition, this series is widely used in training and executive development programs.

Books are priced at $19.95 U.S.
Price subject to change.

To order, call 1-800-668-6780, or go online at www.HBSPress.org

Title	Product #
Harvard Business Review on **Entrepreneurship**	9105
Harvard Business Review on **Finding and Keeping the Best People**	5564
Harvard Business Review on **Innovation**	6145
Harvard Business Review on **Knowledge Management**	8818
Harvard Business Review on **Leadership**	8834
Harvard Business Review on **Leadership at the Top**	2756
Harvard Business Review on **Leading in Turbulent Times**	1806
Harvard Business Review on **Managing Diversity**	7001
Harvard Business Review on **Managing High-Tech Industries**	1828
Harvard Business Review on **Managing People**	9075
Harvard Business Review on **Managing the Value Chain**	2344
Harvard Business Review on **Managing Uncertainty**	9083
Harvard Business Review on **Managing Your Career**	1318
Harvard Business Review on **Marketing**	8040
Harvard Business Review on **Measuring Corporate Performance**	8826
Harvard Business Review on **Mergers and Acquisitions**	5556
Harvard Business Review on **Motivating People**	1326
Harvard Business Review on **Negotiation**	2360
Harvard Business Review on **Nonprofits**	9091
Harvard Business Review on **Organizational Learning**	6153
Harvard Business Review on **Strategic Alliances**	1334
Harvard Business Review on **Strategies for Growth**	8850
Harvard Business Review on **The Business Value of IT**	9121
Harvard Business Review on **The Innovative Enterprise**	130X
Harvard Business Review on **Turnarounds**	6366
Harvard Business Review on **What Makes a Leader**	6374
Harvard Business Review on **Work and Life Balance**	3286

Management Dilemmas: Case Studies from the Pages of Harvard Business Review

How often do you wish you could turn to a panel of experts to guide you through tough management situations? The Management Dilemmas series provides just that. Drawn from the pages of *Harvard Business Review,* each insightful volume poses several perplexing predicaments and shares the problem-solving wisdom of leading experts. Engagingly written, these solutions-oriented collections help managers make sound judgment calls when addressing everyday management dilemmas.

These books are priced at $19.95 U.S.
Price subject to change.

Title	Product #
Management Dilemmas: **When Change Comes Undone**	5038
Management Dilemmas: **When Good People Behave Badly**	5046
Management Dilemmas: **When Marketing Becomes a Minefield**	290X

Harvard Business Essentials

In the fast-paced world of business today, everyone needs a personal resource—a place to go for advice, coaching, background information, or answers. The Harvard Business Essentials series fits the bill. Concise and straightforward, these books provide highly practical advice for readers at all levels of experience. Whether you are a new manager interested in expanding your skills or an experienced executive looking to stay on top, these solution-oriented books give you the reliable tips and tools you need to improve your performance and get the job done. Harvard Business Essentials titles will quickly become your constant companions and trusted guides.

These books are priced at $19.95 U.S., except as noted.
Price subject to change.

Title	Product #
Harvard Business Essentials: **Negotiation**	1113
Harvard Business Essentials: **Managing Creativity and Innovation**	1121
Harvard Business Essentials: **Managing Change and Transition**	8741
Harvard Business Essentials: **Hiring and Keeping the Best People**	875X
Harvard Business Essentials: **Finance**	8768
Harvard Business Essentials: **Business Communication**	113X
Harvard Business Essentials: **Manager's Toolkit ($24.95)**	2896
Harvard Business Essentials: **Managing Projects Large and Small**	3213
Harvard Business Essentials: **Creating Teams with an Edge**	290X

The Results-Driven Manager

The Results-Driven Manager series collects timely articles from *Harvard Management Update* and *Harvard Management Communication Letter* to help senior to middle managers sharpen their skills, increase their effectiveness, and gain a competitive edge. Presented in a concise, accessible format to save managers valuable time, these books offer authoritative insights and techniques for improving job performance and achieving immediate results.

These books are priced at $14.95 U.S.
Price subject to change.

To order, call 1-800-668-6780, or go online at www.HBSPress.org

Readers of the Results-Driven Manager series find the following Harvard Business School Press books of interest.

If you find these books useful:	You may also like these:
Presentations That Persuade and Motivate	Working the Room (8199)
Face-to-Face Communications for Clarity and Impact	HBR on Effective Communication (1437) HBR on Managing People (9075)
Winning Negotiations That Preserve Relationships	HBR on Negotiation (2360) HBE Guide to Negotiation (1113)
Teams That Click	The Wisdom of Teams (3670) Leading Teams (3332)
Managing Yourself for the Career You Want	Primal Leadership (486X) Leading Quietly (4878) Leadership on the Line (4371)

To order, call 1-800-668-6780, or go online at www.HBSPress.org

How to Order

Harvard Business School Press publications are available worldwide from your local bookseller or online retailer.
You can also call

1-800-668-6780

Our product consultants are available to help you
8:00 a.m.–6:00 p.m., Monday–Friday, Eastern Time.
Outside the U.S. and Canada, call: 617-783-7450
Please call about special discounts for quantities greater than ten.

You can order online at

www.HBSPress.org